Kosher Sex

KOSHER SEX

A Recipe for
Passion and Intimacy

Shmuley Boteach

Duckworth

Fourth impression June 1998
First published in May 1998 by
Gerald Duckworth & Co. Ltd.
The Old Piano Factory
48 Hoxton Square, London N1 6PB
Tel: 0171 729 5986
Fax: 0171 729 0015

A catalogue record for this book is available
from the British Library.

ISBN 0 7156 2832 1

Typeset by Ray Davies
Printed and bound in Great Britain by
Redwood Books Ltd, Trowbridge

Contents

Part Three
Sex for Single People

Part Four
Marriage and Divorce

Part Five
Kosher Sex: a Recipe

To my siblings
Sara, Bar Kochva, Chaim Moishe, and Ateret
whose love sustained me through our
parents' turbulent marriage
and divorce.

Acknowledgements

In my previous books, I have always thanked my wife last, in the spirit of saving the best for the summit and conclusion. But any wife who endures a Rabbi-husband who spends a year writing a book about sex deserves to be thanked first. And although by the publication date she will have changed her last name to Debbie Smith and had cosmetic surgery so that none of her friends recognise her, I do want to thank my extraordinary wife for all her devotion and support. Of course, there was that time last week when she yelled at the top of her lungs, 'I've had it with you, I should have listened to my mother. I could have done so much better than you. Johnny, who I dated before you, is now a plumber earning three times your salary. Even your stupid books never sell!' So Debbie, wherever you are, thanks for leaving some cold meatballs in the freezer. They're still keeping me going.

My mother was also scandalised by her Rabbi-son writing a book with this title. So I convinced her that she had misheard, and that the real title of the book was *Kosher Sax*, and concerns itself with the relationship between President Bill Clinton and the American Jewish community. So now she is proudly distributing the book to all her closest friends, telling them that her son is a political theorist. This has still not stopped them, unfortunately, from severing all ties with her ('There goes the mother of that strange Rabbi. Quick, let's cross to the other side.')

Likewise, I would like to thank my six children for all being so well-behaved while this book was written, affording me some peace and quiet to get on with the job. Knowing that Daddy needed some silent time, they reduced their warring and fighting to 60 times per day – from a summer high of 190 – and only interrupted me when the quarrels became really serious – like when baby Shaina was being used as a club by her brother Mendy to clobber older sister Chana into submission.

I, of course, must thank my publisher at Duckworth, the very sensitive and deeply philosophical – and thoroughly decent – Robin Baird-Smith. Robin originally contracted me to write *An Intelligent Person's Guide to Judaism*, which will hopefully be out next year, God willing. When I told him about the book on sex, he accused me of trying to bring all of Duckworth downmarket and into disrepute. But my response, 'Robin, what else is there to life besides the sincere search for celebrity and recognition, and how else will I attain these noble and lofty goals if I don't write about sex?' left him with no proper rejoinder. So what we did, in order to increase sales, is offer three free copies of the Judaism book for every *Kosher Sex* copy sold. (Sadly, even this hasn't worked, and copies of the book are now being distributed free with every lottery ticket sold.)

Special thanks must be given to the excellent editing job by Martin Rynja. I really want to express my appreciation to Martin for actually allowing some of my original manuscript – however small a fraction – into the final, published edition. Martin referred to his having cut out nine-tenths of the manuscript as 'a vast improvement over the original.' But my revenge against Martin should come from the readers themselves. For it was he who removed all the graphic, sexual pictures originally used to better demonstrate key points. Oh well, more room for the imagination. He also sadistically insisted on cutting out the first three hundred pages which contained an exhaustive and detailed description of my early childhood. You'll all just have to wait now for the movie.

I also want to express my appreciation to all of the many friends who shared intimate details of their lives with me for inclusion in this book. You should find it relatively easy to identify them through the thinly disguised veneer I used. Some of them are downright saucy. And who was it that said that Jews have no fun?

Finally, in a moment of complete seriousness, I pay homage to the supreme Master of the Universe, God Almighty, whose infinite love and kindness has always sustained me through the trials of life and existence, and blessed me with a wife and family who never fail to brighten the dark moments. May his Glory be blessed for ever and ever.

February, 1998   Shmuley Boteach

Kosher Sex: the Soul of Marriage

Therefore shall a man leave his father and leave his mother. He shall cleave unto his wife, and they shall become one flesh.

Genesis 2: verse 24

... a more perfect delight when we be naked in each other's arms clasped together toying with each other's limbs, buried in each other's bodies, struggling, panting, dying for a moment. Shall we not feel then, even then, that there is more in store for us, that those thrilling writhings are but dim shadows of a union which shall be perfect?   S. Chitty, *The Beast and the Monk*

Sex is emotion in motion.   Mae West

The person who writes before you is a man deeply influenced by his parent's divorce at the age of eight. As I grew up, I had one great wish that haunted me from that moment. I dreamed that one day that my parents would remarry, and I am sure that the same is true for most other children who witness the break-up of their parent's marriage.

I became a terrible student who didn't want to grow up, spending most of my time angering teachers and leading petty class revolts. A little voice whispered in my ear, 'Why grow up when this is what is in store for you?' I became a young cynic who believed that nothing in life worked out. The world seemed made of incongruent pieces of a broken puzzle that never really fit, and happiness in life seemed as illusory as it was elusive. I remember how at age thirteen at my Bar Mitzvah, when my parents asked me (separately) what I wanted as a present and that I, though being very selfish and materialistic, responded that I wanted them to get back together.

When I was fourteen I gave up on the idea of seeing them together again. That was also the same age at which I entered into the earliest stage of becoming a Rabbi. Since I couldn't bring my parents back together, I became inspired to pursue a profession which was about mending hearts and healing wounds. Now, seventeen years later, I have one strong wish, and that is to try to remain happily married myself, and finding a means of helping others to achieve this dream state.

Feeling special

One of the consequences of being the child of divorce is no longer feeling special. I remember how difficult I found it every time the teacher said, 'Now go home and practice this passage of the Bible tonight with your father.' My father was 3000 miles away and I felt deficient, as if something was wrong with me personally that I couldn't correct.

But, feeling special and unique is one of the single most important human facets. It is part of our survival instinct. No human comes into this world feeling ordinary. The Bible says that every human being is created 'in the image of God,' and what that incredibly powerful verse means is that the same way that God is the one and only – there is no other like Him – every one of us is also the one and only. There is no other like us. In the same way that no two people look the same, no two people are the same. And the essence and ultimate purpose of a relationship is to establish and substantiate that uniqueness. When someone chooses to love you, it can mean only one thing; *that you are worth loving*.

People today appear vulnerable and rudderless. They feel themselves to be trapped in a vast impersonal universe, which is unfeeling and indifferent to them. They move from relationship to relationship, never quite being wholly happy or satisfied. And even when they do find a relationship which brings a measure of happiness, they still complain about not feeling completely understood. Loneliness – the image of a man or a woman sitting at home watching TV on their own – has become the icon of our generation. To counter this atomisation of humanity, G-d gave us marriage, the essence of which is to find a soul-mate who grasps us fully. Someone who even in moments of complete silence still can read our inner soul and accommodate our innate will. Conversely, the nature of loneliness is feeling that there is no-one who will ever fathom the depth of our spirit and recognise our specialness and individuality. Our generation is suffering from a crisis of intimacy, which manifests itself above all else in our not feeling unique.

Twice in my life I remember feeling exceptionally special, as if I were chosen for some great mission. The first time was when I was in boarding school at age 15 and we had a late-night birthday party for a classmate. The boy in question became exceptionally drunk, and started telling me that he is a messenger from God who was sent to tell me that I was the Messiah! 'You have been chosen to redeem the world of its iniquity. You are God's anointed.' I told him he was drunk and should go to sleep. But when he began quoting from obscure Jewish mystical works, proving that my name was alluded to in ancient scripture as the promised redeemer, and began revealing a new and most powerful Cabalistic name of God, everyone who heard him thereafter looked at me reverentially, as if an angel had suddenly appeared. Sadly, the next morning everything he said was proven false (but my mother still thinks he had something there).

And the second time, and by far the most important, was the day I got married and heard how the next morning my wife was being referred to as Mrs Boteach. I couldn't hear enough of it. Here was someone who found me so special that she was prepared to take my last name and share my life. Someone who came home with me every night, and heard my petty complaints about life and work. Someone who found the beauty within me, even when I only saw my ugliness.

Many of us today attempt to substantiate our existence and become special through world-renowned achievement – by becoming millionaires or Prime Ministers. Indeed, every human being is endowed with a feeling of specialness, as though it is they who can save the planet and redeem the world. Yet, not all of us are global Messiahs. Not all of us are great historical figures. But, indeed, we are all personal Messiahs, able to redeem and uplift the lives of those around us who care for us most. My friend in the story above was right about me. I am the Messiah, albeit a small one (both in size and stature). In fact, we all have the power to redeem and save at least one life by choosing them and making them feel wanted and special throughout their lives. This is the beauty of marriage and why it is central to human living.

Marriage is a simple statement of your beloved finding you so special and unique that they would rather spend the vast majority of their remaining time on this earth with you than with any other person. They had the choice to make this commitment to many other people. But they gave the commitment to you because they found you the most special. Now, don't you feel peerless?

Individuality and marriage

Though, it is a source of pride for me to be a family man – for which I am immensely thankful to God, the source of all blessing – this does not mean that for me or any-one else, marriage can always be an easy state of affairs. Indeed, my marriage endures some very stormy moments, the fault of which almost always lies firmly in my court.

I am not the kind of person for whom selflessness comes easy. Less so am I the kind of man who naturally subscribes to the closed limits of an institution. On the contrary, one of the by-products of my parent's divorce was that, in large measure, I had to raise myself and as a consequence became accustomed to near absolute freedom. My mother worked two jobs to support us, which meant that I grew up without much close supervision. Moreover, I am the youngest of five children, spoilt by everyone, and thus not very accustomed to sharing.

Nevertheless, I feel I am one of the people to whom a truth has been revealed gradually, namely, that irrespective of whatever sacrifices marriage entails – and it involves many – marriage and the family are man's greatest source of happiness. No one who marries will ever find someone perfect. In this respect marriage is a statement of deep-seated love for humanity, whereby we love companionship more than we love perfection. Those who hold out for years, dating and discarding people by the dozen, find perfection more tantalising that human company. God created each of us missing an essential something, thereby establishing a life-long dependency between us for someone is prepared to love us in spite of our flaws and compliment our deficiency.

Why take my advice?

My authority for penning a second book on marriage and relationships – my first addressed the issue of maintaining passion in marriage and turning one's marriage into an illicit affair – derives not from any claims or pretensions that I may have toward being an exemplary husband, lover or father. I make no such claims. Indeed, I feel truly humbled when witnessing the countless men who are my superiors in all these departments. Rather, it derives simply from the fact that the pain of my parent's divorce has caused me to become obsessed with the simple question of how a man and a woman might remain together happily for the duration of their lives, and to contribute something positive to the state of marriage and parenthood.

Writing a book of this nature is, furthermore, in a sense therapeutic. When one undergoes traumatic experiences in life, there arises a need to lift the experience from the realm of meaninglessness and try to turn it to something life-affirming and good. Nihilism, or suffering for nothing, holds no attraction for me. If the experiences which I endured can, in some way, help me to help others bolster the success of their marriage and avoid the tragedy of marital discord, then my experience has been redeeming, although certainly not worthwhile.

I am not one of those individuals who believes that pain and suffering are life's greatest tutors. There is no suffering servant who is central to Judaism and on account of whose pain humankind attains redemption. On the contrary, I believe that suffering only causes us to be twisted, angry, scarred, cynical and alone. Whatever greatness which those who have suffered achieve is attained *despite*, and not *because* of the fact, that they have suffered. It is only because we are all bound to ache and grieve at times, given that the world is not yet perfect, that we must, at the very least, integrate these experiences into our lives and allow them to become a blessing by causing others to learn from our pain, without having to endure the same painful experience themselves.

Indeed, as a Rabbi to students and mature community people – both Jewish and non-Jewish – beginning at the University of Oxford and continuing to include London for over a decade, I have witnessed many people in deep pain, much of which has been caused by relationships gone awry. I have sat with husbands and wives who could not help but abuse each other even in my presence, and many wives have asked me advice when they heard of their husband's infidelity. I grew up with a close homosexual friend and watched him struggle with the Herculean task of finding love and companionship, without compromising the essentials of his faith. And I have watched a mother's struggle with the twin tasks of comforting and raising her offspring, while stifling her own pain and loneliness.

But, throughout this period I have sought to identify what makes a marriage work and what destroys its prospects, those actions which bring a couple together, and those which create gulfs and distance. And it has taught me an important lesson. We human beings cannot stop earthquakes and all car accidents. But we can prevent, even to a limited degree, the tragedy of aloneness that affects so many people in the information age, a world in which machines and technology have become ever more alluring than people. There is no need for a society in which images on the television screen constitute the main form of fellowship.

Sewing together two souls as one

The focus of this book is on sex, and the central place it occupies within marriage and relationships. Our generation outwardly aspires to great sex, but inwardly to kosher sex, as I hope to demonstrate. This book is designed to define what kosher sex is and assist the reader in bringing it into his or her life.

I know that sex itself sells and is in great demand. Indeed, the word on the street for the past thirty years is sex, sex, and more sex. That may not be a bad thing. But why do none of our most sophisticated social commentators speak of the possibility that sexual lust is designed to make us dependent on human closeness and warmth in much the same way that it is responsible for the survival of the species? Why does everyone assume that the sexual urge is there merely to be satisfied. Perhaps the purpose of sex is to have us hunger for human company in perpetuity.

It is the central premise of this book that the real, underlying reason we seek sex is not physical pleasure, but emotional intimacy. We do not seek mere orgasms, but rather the incredibly close proximity of another warm human being. And because our sex lives are today not yielding emotional intimacy, we are fast becoming bored with sex. It is becoming an empty experience which leaves no trace and few pleasant memories. Hence, the need for kosher sex.

Here we arrive at a strange paradox. Ours is simultaneously

the most oversexed and yet also the loneliest generation of all time. If sex is physically the closest two people will ever come to each other, why is it not breeding emotional intimacy? How is that two people can share the pleasures of the flesh and still not be tied by the strings of the heart? I speak to young people all the time who tell me that, although they have been dating – or living together – for several years, they still can't get married because they don't feel they know each other well enough yet. 'I still feel unsure about Jerry,' one twenty-seven year-old woman told me of her boyfriend of five years. 'Parts of his personality worry me, even scare me.'

Statements such as these result from the simple fact that, although the Bible refers to physical love as the ultimate form of knowledge, sex today often confuses more than it clarifies. Ask the average young person what their relationship means to them, and you will often receive ambiguous replies. Today's relationships involve very misty definitions. They do not necessarily entail love. Many are of such short duration, or based on convenience, that love is not given the opportunity to flourish. Others will say that their relationship is based on intensity of emotion. But they also concede that one may feel very intensely about a close friend. Still others define a relationship as having sex together. But indeed many people have sex today outside any formal relationship.

Yet, the one thing that everyone repeatedly tells me is that they think the most essential component of a relationship is exclusivity. A relationship today means that you have sex with your partner and with no-one else. And this is what people mean when they say they wish to be in a fulfilling relationship. Above all else they want this very special exclusivity. People are still clamouring, not just for pleasure, but for intimacy in their relationships, but are rarely finding it.

The Wise Man and the Clever Man

An ancient Jewish aphorism declares that the difference between the wise and clever man is that the clever man can extricate himself from a situation into which the wise man would never have got himself into in the first place. Ours is a clever generation, not a wise one. Libraries of self-help books now dot the book-selling landscape giving advice on how to rectify every problem that arises in life and relationships.

Yours sex life has become boring. No problem. Pull out a bull whip, or tie your partner up to the lampshade. Even better, rent a blue video at the local shop with such searing titles as 'Honey, I accommodated the entire neighbourhood'. Your husband ignores you. No problem. Toss the bum out and get yourself a temporary lover to restore your self-confidence.

But our parents and grandparents never had self-help books or other aids. Was it because they weren't interested in personal growth? Or was it because they were wise and took pre-emptive action to forestall problems which they knew might later arise, while we conduct our lives and relationships on a crisis to crisis basis. We are fire-fighters while they were town-planners.

Having spent ten years counselling people on marriage and relationships, I now believe that most of us are crisis workers, not lovers. We have no plan for our intimate lives, so flames erupt in every brush, while we arbitrarily stamp them out. We'd rather rely on our cleverness in extricating ourselves from difficulties presented as and when they arise, rather than confront the issue head on.

Nowhere is this more in evidence than in our attitudes toward sex. We don't know what quite to make of it. Is it something we should do, watch on TV, discuss, ignore, indulge, or suppress? Sex at once excites us, compels us, rules us, yet also bores us, provoking yawns and serving as the butt of jokes. Boys and girls today begin having sex in their tender teens, yet seemed disillusioned – weary and worn out – by the time they hit their twenties.

Studies show that most women who begin having sex in their mid-teens do so, not for pleasure, but because they fear the ridicule of prudishness. The 1948 Kinsey Report on male sexuality found that for 75 per cent of American men intercourse lasted no more than two minutes. A recent survey by New York University's sleep disorders centre has found that more than five million Americans habitually fall asleep while making love. (The report did not reveal whether their partner noticed any difference in their performance.) Sex has become like running water. Now that it is available on tap, we take it for granted and give it little thought. It is truly a crime that the highest form of human bonding is given scant thought by intelligent adults.

Yet simply put, sex is the single most important means of keeping a man and woman happily under the same roof together for a lifetime. Libraries of studies show that couples who have healthy love lives also have healthy marriages. Furthermore, sex is the only human undertaking which, when done right, rids us of all inhibition and manifests our innermost essence. As such, it is the ultimate form of knowledge. No other component of a relationship is better suited toward making two adults feel intensely good about one another, and no other subject therefore requires more wisdom and guidance, especially since it is so naturally prone to selfishness and abuse.

Marriage counsellors and sex gurus have even given up on the centrality of sex within marriage. Communication – talking things through – has become the mantra of the age. But the ignorance of sex, far from being innocent, has serious repercussions. Foremost among them is the loss of intimacy, the primary cause of which is our total lack of understanding of sex. We are all making love with our bodies, but not with our minds or our souls. Hence, the wellsprings of sexual knowledge have dried up, and what remains is a dead and lifeless corpse, which is how we feel the morning after, when ensconced in a non-loving relationship.

Why Judaism?

While I am a Rabbi and this book does contain the word 'Kosher' in its title, it is not a book that draws only on Jewish sources and wisdom. Less so is it a book meant only for Jews. Rather, the essentially Jewish grounding of the book derives from Judaism's unique qualifications to discuss both sex and relationships. Unlike other religious traditions, Judaism has never had a prudish or conservative sexual ethic. On the contrary, Judaism has always celebrated the commitment that exists between a loving man and woman. The physical component of commitment has often served for the Cabalists (Jewish mystics) as a metaphor of the love and interaction between God and man.

Long ago, well before Christianity enacted legislation forbidding its clerics from marrying or having sex, the ancient Rabbis were giving explicit sexual advice to married men and women as to how they could enjoy pleasurable, yet holy, intimate relations.

The Rabbis made female orgasm an obligation incumbent on every Jewish husband. No man was allowed to use a woman merely for his own gratification.

Of course, one might reject the need for any religious guidance or pronouncements on sex in favour of a totally liberal sexual ethic which has no rules or impediments. But a sexual life without rules leads to the debasement and depersonalisation of sex, where long-term love and pleasure is substituted with short-term sensual indulgence which ultimately deadens our sexuality and leads us to treat our own bodies with contempt. A greater appreciation for conversation in marriage rather than physical love is the next logical step.

Rather than offering prescriptive rules about sex and marriage, Judaism offers guidelines, or what might be called *erotic channels of communication*, designed not to circumscribe our sexual routine, but to focus it and make it potent, so that sex becomes passionate and effective in conjuring up long-term emotions and commitment. Neither does Judaism indulge in guilt, harping on one's sexual past or sins. Sex is a motion designed to engender deep and lasting emotions.

On the contrary, the essence of Jewish thought is *gei veiter*, always move forward. Never become mired in your past. Possessed deep within the infinite soul of man is the opportunity to reinvent himself constantly. We can always reclaim our innocence. Whatever man has done in the past, tomorrow brings a new day with limitless capacity for a new beginning in human relationships. Judaism is not out to condemn man for his sexual nature or his love for sensual pleasure, but rather to uplift man from the realm of the animal so that he enjoys human sexual relations, as opposed to ridding himself of a biological urge. Even marriages that appear dormant, like an inactive volcano, can greatly benefit from ancient Rabbinical advice about how to rekindle the lamp of erotic passion in one's relationship.

An often overlooked fact is a further reason that relationships require wisdom rather than cleverness. Every marriage involves the orchestration of two polar opposites. For any relationship to be successful, it must perforce embody two contradictory extremes. One is passion, the other is intimacy. One is a love like fire, the other a love like water, and there's the rub, because the two are, of course, mutually exclusive. Couples desire not only to be lovers, but also best friends. They wish to enjoy a passionate and exciting sex life, but also wish for the tranquillity and soothing qualities of life-long companionship. Sure, a woman sometimes wants her husband to throw her onto the kitchen table and make passionate love, but she also wants to come home nights and curl up with a book next to her comforting husband and a warm fireplace. We sometimes love running away to Paris for the weekend. But we also want to come home to our own place and have somebody waiting for us. We desire novelty, but also predictability.

The instant availability of sex has undermined both these key marital ingredients. Immediate sexual gratification is the destroyer of passion, excitement, and eroticism, while sex with many partners and exposure to endless explicit sexual images is the destroyer of intimacy. What I will explore throughout this book is the kind of sex that serves to fill this purpose of bringing together these opposites of passion and intimacy, and the kind that doesn't. Few sexual matters of substance will escape our scrutiny. Is there a sexual position that is most conducive to greater intimacy? We will ask how sex can best be employed to smooth over the jagged edges of a relationship, and whether sex should be used to end arguments. This is a real sore point between an overwhelming percentage of women who wish to talk things through, and the men in their lives who would much rather kiss and make up. Is it proper for husbands and wives to have sex when they are angry with each other? Is it appropriate for sex sometimes to be used as a weapon? For instance, should a woman withhold sex until she gets here way in marriage, especially when she feels that her husband is being utterly insensitive to her feelings and needs.

Because sex is the central key in engendering emotional intimacy, the focus of this book is on sex and familiarity and warmth which it engenders. First it offers a perspective on sex and its purpose. It them looks at sexual technique, with specific emphasis on those that engender intimacy. Which sexual positions are most conducive to bringing two people emotionally together? Is masturbation an impediment to marital unity? What of pornography and prostitution? Is it true that marriage is a killer of passion and intimacy? Why is sex the most pleasurable human experience? Why is sex in the dark so much more personal than

sex with the lights on? Is oral sex kosher sex? What constitutes
sexual deviance? Will sex before marriage have any bearing on
our ability to create long-lasting ties with members of the opposite sex?

Most married couples today are either lovers or great friends

In counselling couples I witness two types of marriage. In the first
type, a couple are the best of friends. They share every secret and
can read each other's minds, knowing every thought before it is
even expressed. They are trusted companions who stick together
through all of life's vicissitudes. The problem: they have little or
no passion. They are best friends, but not lovers. The second type
of marriage is fiery, both for good and for bad. A couple are lovers.
There is much excitement in the marriage, but they fight a lot as
well. They shout and argue and make up with passionate love.
Their marital flame burns too brightly. Rarely do we see marriages that somehow straddle these two opposites and unite the
best aspects of both. The purpose of this book, then, is to show
how to bring into marriage the kind of positive feelings and
warmth that only sex can induce and only friendship can sustain.
Amidst the parched and arid desert of contemporary loveless,
casual, and arbitrary sex, there exists a cool oasis of soothing and
refreshing waters which drip from intensely intimate human
encounters, creating a paradise of happy and passionate romance. This book is written to counter the drying up of the
wellsprings of sexual knowledge, leading to Eden, a place of
happiness and intimacy.

Part One

The Sex File

1. Lust and commitment

Yes, sex without love is an empty experience. But as empty experiences go, it's one of the best. Woody Allen

Marriage is like a three ring circus. First the engagement ring, second the wedding ring, and third the suffer-ring.

Anonymous

At the heart of all our lives lies a strong and potent mystery. Michael Jackson steps off an aeroplane in Eastern Europe and thirty thousand fans await his arrival. He feels mighty special. They all want him and shout his name. They've taken off from their work to greet and cheer his arrival. But then, off the same airline steps Mr Jones. There aren't thirty thousand people waiting for him to disembark. In fact, there is only one woman – Mrs Jones whose been waiting for her husband to return home. And while everyone walks by, even when Michael Jackson himself walks by, she ignores them all. To her, Mr Jones is even more important, more thrilling, than the world's biggest pop star. And when Mr Jones reaches the arrivals gate and sees his wife's smile and excitement, he feels as special as she does.

How can everyday, ordinary people, become so special to one another? When I was a child, I saw Muhammad Ali walking in Miami Beach. I got his autograph and ran home to ask my mother if we could invite him home for dinner. But that night my older brother was returning from boarding school, and my mother was preparing a big dinner in his honour. 'I don't need Muhammad Ali at the table, Shmuley. I am much more excited that your brother will be here.' Why would a mother want to see her ordinary son rather than dine with the world's greatest sportsman? The answer, of course, is love. Love has the power to

transform the ordinary into the extraordinary and magical. Or,
even better stated, love has the power to unearth and reveal how
all people really are special. Love not only gives us wings. It gives
us vision.

The fear of commitment

Yet, nowadays people, particularly young people, shun commitment. They prefer sex to love, and therefore never achieve this
vision. I've watched countless young couples date at Oxford and
fall in love. Some undergraduates date and remain loyal to each
other the length of their three years at Oxford, and a great many
of the graduate students live together while at Oxford. In many
cases they also come from traditional homes, and yet they still
don't contemplate marriage, preferring to remain somewhat un-
committed. Marriage seems to have become the ultimate modern
heresy.

I often ask them why not? If this is the person you love, and
you agree that they are marriage material, why not marry? Why
not have someone who chooses to be with you above everyone
else, thus perennially making you feel unique and unbreakable,
untouchable and undefeatable? They then give a myriad of re-
sponses, but the most common one is, as one student put it: 'You
can't marry and expect someone else to fulfil you. You've got to do
it yourself. You first have to grow and develop on your own. You
have to know who you are. Only then can you join with someone
else and seek to build something.' Their mindset is that growth,
happiness and contentment is primary an inner, solitary experience. And why shouldn't it be?

Love not war

There is an unshakeable belief that the world around is getting
better and better and more at peace with itself. The possibility of
a world war today is completely remote, the spread of liberal
democracy continues, and nations are working together in new
economic communities as well as contributing large sums to
poorer countries in foreign aid. In our personal lives we all want
a slice of this fabulous freedom too. With all those things out of

the way we would be mad not to want to realise the opportunities that previous generations could only dream of.

Yes, we are willing to concede that the technology available to us to master our world doesn't make our lives easier so much as challenge us on to ever more ambitious projects of achievement. The exertion of effort, say, to communicate with people around the world is nowhere near as trying as it was just half-a-century ago. But, those who own portable phones, and are therefore effectively on call 24-hours-a-day, can testify to the entrapment, rather than the convenience, that modern living affords. It's all part of the game, for we don't want to miss our connection to go up to the next level of play. Who needs someone who might slow us down?

Sex as a basic necessity

And anyway aren't love and sex one and the same, a biological necessity like food. Our hormones and genes force us into sex. Our bodies forever feel they need sensual pleasure and sexual release, and so we find someone and we copulate. In the famous rape trial of William Kennedy Smith in Palm Springs, Florida, Smith, who was acquitted, took the stand and was questioned by his attorney, Robert Black who asked him whether he had made love to the victim. He answered, 'Bob, you're a little old-fashioned. I wouldn't say we made love. Rather, we had sex.' Sex is no more than an urge and so young people just say they're horny as if just to say they are hungry.

Here too science comes to our aid. Evolutionists would describe this urge as being responsible for the survival of the species. The sex-drive is nature working to guarantee the widest possible distribution of the organism's gene pool thus ensuring the survival of the species. Far from being an act of love, it is an act of survival. It is a momentary interruption of the war between the sexes by a mutual truce between man and woman for the higher goal of human maintenance and continuity.

Robert Wright, author of *The Moral Animal*, captures this feeling brilliantly: 'The feeling of hunger, no less than the stomach, is here because it helped keep our ancestors alive long enough to reproduce and rear their young. Feelings of lust, no less than the sex organs, are here because they aided reproduction directly. Any ancestors who lacked stomachs or hunger or sex organs or lust – well, they wouldn't have become ancestors, would they?'

Sex is not a trivial mathematical equation

But, honestly, who really buys all this? Am I the only one who feels slightly uncomfortable about the analogy between sex and our bowels. What of emotional hunger? A friend once told me that for the last two years of her marriage she had withheld sex from her husband because every night he would merely climb on and off of her so that she was made to feel that he 'was going to the bathroom on top of me, and as soon as he was relieved I was discarded and he fell asleep.' Would our response be any different. Would anyone's hunger for sex really be satisfied if our spouse treated us that way?

Sex does not merely involve the transfer of seed from male to female as part of the food chain. Eating is something we do by and for ourselves. But the deposition of semen comes about through the closest possible human contact known to mankind. Food makes us dependent on nothing more than inanimate objects, but sex transcends by far the biological fact of reproduction. Sex makes us hunger for people. We cannot reproduce without another person and thus the fact of the survival of the human race is inextricably linked with the fact of humanity as a family, human closeness, human warmth, and human intimacy. Sex is not a chemical formula. It is simply the only human activity which physically necessitates another human being.

The objective truth about sex

And let's not kid ourselves. We are not the sex-crazed society that we pretend to be, and if we are, it is only in speech, not action. Certainly, everywhere we look there is sex: in films, television, newspapers, and magazines, and a recent study shows that the average man thinks of sex some six times per hour. Yet, the only place where it is really absent is in the bedroom. Contemporary studies show that people are having very little sex these days, and that young single people have far less sex than married people.

According to *Sex in America*, the most comprehensive sexual survey ever carried out, '36 per cent of men age eighteen to twenty four had no sex with a partner in the past year or had sex just a few times. 27 per cent of women in that age group show similar patterns ... For women aged thirty and up, more are not having partnered sex than are having it. More than 4 in 10 women age fifty five to sixty five had no sexual partners, and an astonishing 70 per cent of women in their seventies were no longer having partnered sex.'

Nor are people really enjoying sex much either. Women report enjoying sex less than 30 per cent of the time, whereas men report being pleased only 47 per cent of the time. According to *Sex in America*, the entire presumption that our society and generation are saturated with sex is all a sham: 'The general picture of sex with a partner in America shows that Americans do not have a secret life of abundant sex. If nothing else, the startlingly modest amounts of partnered sex reveal how much we as a society can deceive ourselves about other people's sex lives.'

Sex draws men and women together, love turns it into commitment

And you may agree that we are not as sex-driven as we say we are. Nonetheless, you may say, who needs commitment when sex or, better, lust alone pulls us to share our live with others? Isn't that enough in itself? Why, if our hormones compel us toward other people, what do we need emotion and love for?

There are two answers to that, one simple one and the other profound. The simple answer is this: we can't always have sex, so it is an ineffective way of keeping people together. People can't be at it 24 hours a day, seven days a week (not all of us are Italian). We have to support ourselves and our families. And we are also incapable of living in continual sexual anxiety and expectation. The world would be an awful place if men and women could relate to each other only as potential sexual partners. But we can always be in love, even when separated by a vast geographical distance. Love is much more spiritual than sex.

But, this reason deals with expediency alone. Far more important is the fact that sex is indiscriminate. Love is not. Sex pulls us toward other people *in general* and there are plenty of people who are willing to have sex with just about anyone. Sex requires no particular person. But love draws us to one person in particular, and renders our life meaningless when that person is not part of it. Sex, then, accounts for human reproduction, while love accounts for the unique human ability to build a family and a home, and subsequently a society and a civilisation. Sex certainly guarantees the propagation of the species, but love guarantees that those people will live together in groups. It is love which makes marriage, and not sex.

So, why do we need sex at all? Why not have only love? This is because love can only be sustained by constant sexual interaction. Only sex has the power to call forth our deepest, most powerful emotions. Sex at its best is where a couple are overwhelmed by a tidal wave of positive physical sensations which makes them feel intensely good about each other, and thus causes them to bond. That is, so long as it is kosher sex. And now you see the magnitude of the problem: sex today is primarily about ignoring emotion. Sex is seen as merely a bodily function which needs to be serviced. Sex is for the purpose of pleasure only, without any commitment. We ignore the mystery and consciously stifle the strings of attachment that naturally follow in the wake of the sexual experience. People not only have sex in spite of a lack of emotion, they do so with the express purpose of suppressing emotion. They wish to remain non-committed. This is definitely unsafe, unkosher sex, because it represses the natural response that sex is meant to elicit. Sex and commitment are the ultimate forms of human closeness, and we cannot be close and distant at the same time.

2. Sex and doing what's expected

As bees their sting, so the promiscuous leave behind them in each encounter something of themselves by which they are made to suffer.
                                                                    Cyril Connolly

That woman speaks eighteen languages and can't say No in any of them.
                                                                    Dorothy Parker

Sex – the poor man's polo.
                                                                    Clifford Odets

Judging from my counselling experience it is women who are most hurt by the casualness and callousness of modern sex.

Young women in particular seem to feel that they have to do what is expected of them. This realisation struck me most forcefully when I received a phone call one evening from a close friend in Oxford asking if I could meet that night with a young woman of nineteen who was so depressed she threatened to commit suicide. 'What is the cause or nature of her depression,' I asked. 'It's better if she tells you herself,' my friend replied, 'as it is of a very personal nature and she has to want to tell you.'

So there I was at eight o'clock at night in a friend's house with a girl who looked completely distraught, as if her life were at an end. She introduced herself meekly and for a long time we sat there in silence as I waited for her to say something.

'What's wrong?,' I finally asked. 'Did you have a fight with your parents? Have you split up with a boyfriend? Have you lost your job? Do you need money?' She ignored my questions. Finally, after a prolonged silence, she responded, 'No! But it does have something to do with my boyfriend, or at least my former boyfriend.' 'What?' I pressed the question. 'Did he beat you? Was he unfaithful. Please tell me what's the matter?' 'It's none of that', she replied. 'I caught something from him. I discovered last week that I am HIV positive.'

Her words hit me like a bombshell. Oxford is not a sheltered city, and having served for ten years as Rabbi to the students of the University, there is little I haven't already heard or seen. I have met several gay men, mostly in their thirties and forties, who were either HIV positive or had actual AIDS. But this just seemed very different. This girl was just a kid. Yet she had already contracted the most dreaded disease of the age. 'Are you still with this boyfriend? Does he know?' I said.

'Actually,' she looked up from the table she had been staring at until now, 'I'm not sure which boyfriend it was. It could be one of eleven men that I've been with in the past year.' I tried hard not to raise my eyebrows. 'But you're only nineteen. From what age did you start having sex?' I asked her. 'I started late,' she said 'I was seventeen. But I made up a lot of lost time quickly. I had a lot of men and I wasn't careful about protection or disease. My attitude was that it would never happen to me.'

She sighed, then continued. 'Isn't it ironic that from an act of love such torment can follow.' 'Is that why you had sex with them? So many of them? Because you loved them?' I asked. 'Of course not! Sex is just something you experiment with, you know, for fun,' she said, still gazing down at the floor. I came away from that meeting with a deep sense of sadness. Not only because a young flower was being cut off in its bloom, but also because it had all been for nothing. After the bad news her mental state was of course very low. But the depth of her despair resulted from the realisation that in some way she had parted cheaply of something valuable.

Sex and a feeling of loss

Other women have confirmed this. One woman whom I knew from Oxford as a student told us that she has now been to bed with over twenty guys – got naked with them, as she put it – by her count, all in a fruitless effort to find love with any one of them, and it just never seems to happen. She is attractive, intelligent, well-educated, and she would love to fall in love and get married. But she doesn't seem to stick to anyone after sex and no one seems to stick to her either. The sex is pleasurable, but not warm or intimate. She has yet to transform a casual sexual encounter into an intense and fulfilling relationship.

Another female student said that at the age of twenty she had undertaken the goal of sleeping with a man in every one of the fifty United States. Although she only managed thirty-eight as of this writing, she too pointed out that the more men she slept with, the more having sex was no bigger a decision than going to a film. Thus, as the project had lost its appeal, she gave up.

The rub for men

But men suffer equally. It may well be that we are naturally inclined to sex as a disposable, biological obsession. Let's face it. One minute our skin is tingling and our tongues are sweeping the carpet. But the very moment after sexual satisfaction has been achieved, we are as interested in our sexual partner as we are in going to the dentist's chair. Sleep is all we can think of.

Nonetheless, we pay the price in a different currency. I have met too many husbands who justified having affairs because their wives didn't want sex or were bored of it, and who later discovered that the wives themselves were having a steamy affair, much to their shock. Their wives, they discovered, were bored of sex because of their husband's neglect. 'I honestly didn't believe that she had it in her. I would never have suspected it. My wife's just not the type.'

And there are enough men who have doubts about their active 'biological' life. One handsome and highly successful investment banker, who had taken scores of women to bed, once called me on the morning after yet another conquest, 'Shmuley,' he said 'if I do this just one more time I will not be able to look at myself in the mirror. I woke up this morning trembling and I still can't explain why.'

Back to basics

Our modern mindset does not seem to get us very far. What few of us realise today is that the yearning for emotional intimacy is as real as the hunger for food and water, shelter and clothing. Animals may copulate and then separate, but humans are radically different. We have sex with our minds wide awake. What goes on in our body is not enough. We neglect an essential part of ourselves if we reduce sex to something that is not intimate but merely biological compunction. In fact, we harm ourselves with our casual approach to sex.

There are three possibilities as to what sex is about: pleasure, procreation, or oneness. Judaism, believing that the path to holiness is always found in the 'golden middle,' rejects the far-right extreme of sex-is-only-for-babies. Neither does Judaism embrace the extreme secular view that sex is for fun and pleasure. Rather, Judaism says that the purpose of sex is synthesise and orchestrate two strangers together as one. Sex is the ultimate bonding process. God, in his infinite kindness, gave a man and a woman who are joined together in matrimonial holiness the most pleasurable possible way to call forth their capacity of joining onto another human being and feeling permanently attached.

What we have forgotten is that sex faces us with a choice. If we do it right sex is a technique based on a profound understanding of ourselves, in much the same way that food may be kosher or unkosher. A Jew is commanded to eat kosher food (prepared according to Biblical guidelines) because it is this kind of food that serves to elevate the human condition to a higher spiritual plane and to draw him closer to God. Similarly, in the same way that a human does not stick his head into a trough the same way that a horse would, he does not and should not copulate the way animals do. Intimate sex done right elevates what can be an indulgent, animalistic human practice to a higher plane where we realise the full glory of being human. As the Bible says, 'A man shall leave his father and his mother, he shall cleave unto his wife (have sex with her) and they shall become one flesh.'

Our mind needs to be at the centre of someone else's universe. This is what we have to admit to ourselves. All we want deep down is to be sun kings or queens like Louis XIV of France. We all want to be the sun with a planet revolving around us. We need a human being who cherishes and desires us above all others in order to survive, live, prosper, and contribute to the world that particular gift that only we can give. We need to rise to this challenge if we want to reach our destination as humans. We are all obligated, as the ancient Rabbis wrote two thousand years ago, to feel, even to proclaim, that: 'The world was created for me.'

Marriage is the ultimate setting for this commitment to our lover. In it we can always feel to be loved and never know loneliness, and feel almost as special as the Almighty Himself. Through the unique set up of marriage, bonding two people in a bulwark against the rest of the world, we are assured that we are irreplaceable and a key part of the world, the world we have claimed for ourselves. This is the source of marriage's sanctity, security, and holiness. We are the sun, and our spouse is the planet which revolves around us and basks in our light, in the same way that we are part of our spouse's universe. But, it is up to us to recognise this commitment. And act upon it.

3. The real power of sex

Love is the delusion that one woman differs from another.

H L Mencken

Is sex dirty? Only if it's done right! Woody Allen

When I'm good I'm good. But when I'm bad, I'm even better.

Mae West

Once my wife and I were sitting in a restaurant with a close, female friend, who lamented the break-up of her latest relationship. 'Once we started having sex together – and we waited a month before that happened – the whole thing got so complicated,' she said. 'But that's also when I started loving him more, and becoming more attached.' She then claimed to have the power of doing something extraordinary: 'I can even look around the room and see exactly which couples in this restaurant are having sex and which aren't. You can tell by all the little things.'

'Big deal.' I said. 'You can do that only because everyone is having sex. Hey, this is the 90s! All you got to do is look around and anyone whose pulse hasn't stop beating, or looks like a geek sitting having dinner working with his laptop, or is under thirteen years of age, is definitely having sex!' But she was undaunted.

'Very funny. But I am serious. You can see if they are having sex by how close they feel to each other. How they look at each other, how they speak to each other; even how they argue. People who are having sex are just that much more intimate, even if to them it is only fun. Why do you think that women try and avoid, or feel embarrassed when bumping into men they have slept with in the past? Because they feel too intimate, as if the guy knows something about them that no one else does. You immediately try to avoid eye-contact.'

Sex changes us

Now I didn't exactly get up and go around from table to table asking the couples, 'Hey, my friend and I have a bet on. Can you just tell us, please, are you sleeping together?,' but I do believe that she is absolutely right and that it is discernible. Sex is much more powerful than 'fun,' for recreation leaves no trace. One can spend all night playing video games having fun, but in the morning the experience, except for red eyes, will be utterly forgotten. Sex is different. Two human beings don't become entangled and then disentangle so easily.

Yet, this power of sex is today's lost continent. We said earlier that too many single, young people today don't know more about sex than that it is related to physical lust. If you ask them what sex does, they won't even understand the question. 'Why,' they answer, you have sex to have fun, no? Pleasure! To gratify your sex drive. What else is there to it? Inside of marriage the situation isn't much better. Husbands and wives will have sex as part of their daily, weekly, monthly, or annual (oh my!) routine. One husband even explained to me how the nightly sex of marriage is far superior as a tranquilliser to the sleeping tablets he used to take as a bachelor (did his wife notice?). Another woman – whose husband comes home very late every night from work – told me that she doesn't mind her husband's nightly need for sex, just so long as it doesn't wake her up. 'He's very good about letting me sleep.'

What sex does

Even intelligent and erudite people are clueless what sex is really about. I saw this most pointedly in an article by the usually more sober *Time* magazine writer Barbara Ehrenreich; an essay which I found as deep as a puddle in the crack of a footpath. Mrs Ehrenreich argued that sex is about fun and she was pleased that the population explosion that had excited world fears about over-population would now change the long-held position that sex was about procreation. The whole subject would revert back to its most important phase: that sex is a big game. 'Sex, in our over-populated world, is best seen as a source of fun.' It's one thing to argue that 'sex should be separated from the all-too-serious business of reproduction.' It is quite another, however, to consign it to the ranks of Sega and Nintendo.

Only AIDS and the phenomenal increase in teenage pregnancy (in the UK the highest in Europe) seem to have added a somewhat sharper edge to this pandemic light-heartedness. And yet, they too merely confirm the non-emotional, purely biological state of sex. As Marlon Brando said, 'I don't think I was constructed to be monogamous. I don't think it's the nature of *any* man to be monogamous ... Men are propelled by genetically ordained impulses over which they have no control to distribute their seed into as many females as possible.' Moreover, because sexual disease are 'objective' risks widely covered in the media, they steal the attention from the other, more invisible sexual disease, namely, that an abundance of sexual partners seriously impairs our ability to sustain intimacy when we wish it so.

Don't get me wrong. Sex is probably just as pleasurable today as it was in days gone by. It is also probably just as powerful, and occupies the thoughts of men and women as much as it did previously, if not more. But what sex has *seemingly* lost is an ability to make a man and a woman feel intensely about one another and closer to each other. Stated in other words, it appears as though sex today rarely has the capacity to change the way a man and a woman feel about one another. It is pleasurable and enjoyable while it lasts, but quickly dissipates shortly thereafter.

My students bear this out constantly. Andrew and Shirley met at an Oxford pub and felt instantly attracted to each other. They spoke for hours until they were turned out at the 11pm curfew. They went to Shirley's college room and, eventually, ended up in bed, spending a passionate night together. In the morning, Andrew kissed her on the cheek and said he'd call. Two days later they bumped into each other on the street. Andrew was friendly and very polite, but nothing more. 'Let's meet up again soon,' he yelled as he ran to catch a bus. But Shirley was devastated. 'Did nothing happen two nights ago?' she asked herself.

The psychology of sex

Here lies the problem. We give indiscriminately and then naively expect things to sort themselves according to which of our expectations we choose to fasten upon our gift. The hurricane of explicitness that has, as a result, ravaged our inner hearts and concomitantly our intimate relationships is, however, always attributed to other causes. I have grown weary of hearing endless sex experts explain how the high divorce rate is due to the fact that women are no longer financially dependent on men, or that the growing weakness of patriarchy has contributed to a more liberated female mindset, or that the loss of intimacy in society can easily be repaired with the two greatest buzzwords of all of today's relationships experts: greater communication. Libraries are filled with nonsense spoken by experts.

Saying that women have greater financial freedom and will therefore refuse to remain in a loveless marriage does not explain how that marriage became loveless in the first place. Relationships work on basics and fundamentals, so many of which have been lost, and our hearts have been broken in the process. One of those basics is the exclusivity of sex and hence its intimacy when shared between a loving man and woman. Every sexual survey ever done has shown the same result: the more sexual partners you have before marriage, the greater the chance of divorce – exponentially! Too many cooks spoil the broth and too many sexual partners spoil the bond.

The spell cast by history

The culprit in all this is the Western Romantic ideal, which says that ideally love leads to sex. Through sharing experiences, showing one another consideration, gentleness, and warmth, would-be lovers slowly fall in love. And then, after love has ensued, it leads on to the sexual climax, the apogee of the relationship. Every great classical love story involves these stages: the sexual act is, in the Western romantic view, the consummation of love. And the operative word really is to 'consummate.' Sex is the summit of male/female relationships. Love would be incomplete without out it. Before the act there is *love*, but only sex can elevate it to the next level: *making love*.

To Jews this is completely unintelligible. The Bible's says about the first human coupling: 'Adam came to know his wife Eve.' Prior to their physical coupling, they may have known each other but they were only acquaintances. There was no love. No one within the Jewish community would so degrade love as to claim that it can be possibly formed first, in so short a period of time, and secondly, without direct physical contact.

Even if they were best friends, they were only acquainted with their externalities. They did not possess the kind of knowledge which linked and hooked them together forever. They knew only each other's most revealed aspects. They knew what kind of cuisine the other liked, the holiday destination each preferred, who their favourite artists were, and which music they most enjoyed listening to. They even knew the main issues that troubled their childhood and how the other got along with their respective parents. In short, they knew what the other *did*, but did not know what the other *was*. They didn't know how the other would behave when all inhibition and social adjustment had been surrendered.

Love came only through physical intimacy. As Adam and Eve took off all their outer garments and inner restraints and behaved around one another in the exact same fashion in which they behaved around themselves, that was the moment when they came to know each other. Only then did they fathom one another's essence, peering deep beneath the outer layers into the heart and through the windows of the soul.

The power of carnal knowledge

As a Chassidic Jew I feel this even more keenly. We marry after a short courtship. My wife and I, for example, were introduced, as is the Chassidic Jewish custom, by a mutual friend. I had known Debbie's parents in Australia, and had heard many complimentary things about her (what else would you expect a mother to say?). On our first date, I was 21 and she was 19. We were both shy (OK, OK, I wasn't, she was. But I pretended to be shy since I believe shyness is a great virtue). It was the first time we had ever dated. For four weeks we drove around New York and Miami, sharing drinks and dinners, discussing every subject under the sun, getting to know one another. We then made our decision. We would marry. We had not yet held hands and we shared no physical intimacy until the wedding night (yes, it was a major bummer).

The reasons for this emphasis on brevity of courtship are best explained where the Bible says: 'Isaac then brought her into his mother Sarah's tent, and took Rebecca, and she became his wife; and he loved her.' First, a man and a woman meet. They do not necessarily know how attractive they will prove to one another. However, assuming that they meet and everything goes well, they continue to see one another for a period of time, say a few weeks or even a few months, and then they decide on marriage.

Do they love each other? Probably not. They might feel very attracted to, and have strong feelings for, one another. But on their wedding night it all happens, aided and abetted by sex. They unite in carnal knowledge for the first time. And it is this potency and power of this physical act, which they are both discovering for the first time, which is truly explosive and engenders a pleasurable love appropriate to marriage bridging the chasm that once separated them. They feel no need to restrain or suppress the natural glue that sex conjures up, for they have already committed themselves to one another. From there it can only increase and grow, as they begin to share a life together, build a family, and undertake mutual goals for personal and the public good.

Sex is meant to make two people become one

This belief finds a perfect expression in a Dutch slang-word for sex, *naaien*, which is also the word for sewing. Two garments are put together side by side so that they touch, and a strong thread is pulled and passed between them by a needle that will keep them secure and fastened to one another long after the sewing is over and the weaver is gone. It is thus not the fact of the sewing itself that later ensures that they do not come apart, but rather the after-effects of the sewing, namely the stitched thread that remains strung between them that has made them both into one garment. And the same is true of sex. Repeated acts of lovemaking ensure that the threads are tightened, secured, and strengthened.

This thread is also what ultimately curbs the predatory side of husbands. The love which is engendered means that his wife is always on his mind. He could no more invite a woman back to his empty hotel room than he could invite that same woman into his marital bed in his wife's presence. In his heart and mind, his marriage and the beautiful moments he has shared with his wife make him feel as though she is with him and attached to him always.

Stated in other words, the love engendered by sex within marriage can be so consuming that it devours all of the husband.

In this state there is simply nothing of him left to share with anyone else. He feels that every part of himself is committed, and when he sees a very attractive woman, rather than think of the sexual possibilities which she presents, he is immediately reminded of his wife. It strengthens his ravishing lust for her. And she, responding to the powerful focus and concentration which her husband has for her, responds in kind by becoming the most devoted and loving companion.

4. The myth of compatibility

I love her too, but our neuroses just don't match.

Arthur Miller

To be happy with a man you must understand him a lot and love him a little. To be happy with a woman you must love her a lot and not try to understand her at all. Helen Rowland

The most common error made in matters of appearance is the belief that one should disdain the superficial and let the true beauty of one's soul shine through. If there are places on your body where this is a possibility, you are not attractive— you are leaking.

Fran Lebowitz

I hear you say, but what about sexual compatibility? The argument (which is so important in relationships today) goes that a couple must have sex before marriage to discover whether or not they are sexually suitable. What is even more preferable is for each to have sex with various partners before marriage in order to ensure that the person you will marry is tailor-made sexually. It is extremely important, apparently, since different people have different sexual metabolisms. One person who enjoys sex all the time might end up marrying someone with little or no interest in sex.

This opinion is deeply entrenched nowadays and is defended even if it flies in the face of experience. When I once complimented one of our married Oxford students on how perfectly suited he and his wife seemed, he replied, 'We met at sixteen and dated for five years straight. She was my high school sweetheart. But when I was twenty two we broke up at my instigation. I wanted to marry her but I wanted to be sure that she and I were right, and since she was the only woman I had had sex with, I had to find some other women just to try it out. I suggested to her that she do the same, but she refused, and till today I remain the only guy she's been with. Eventually, after four or five other girlfriends, I concluded that I loved her far more, and we had a special sexual chemistry. Hence the reason for why we now get along so well. It wasn't an accident, you know.'

Sex is indiscriminate

I don't get that. To me his relationship with his wife-to-be survived despite his dalliances, and not because of them. In Judaism, the basic belief is that physical intimacy between a man and a woman is strong enough to conjure up and sustain emotional intimacy. Sexual compatibility is a red herring. Sex on its own is strong enough to engender and force a significant reaction, a veritably a transformation in character and status. For any couple it can create that rhythm that makes sex into a responsive act of love. The only difference is that with some their sexual side is naturally manifest, while others need it to be more revealed by their partners bringing it out through intense affection.

Sexual compatibility is something that must be worked on by heaping love and attention on one's lover. Every woman can be an enchantress and every man a Casanova. If your wife isn't, you ignored her and allowed your attention to be focused on other women, even when you were in her presence. She turned off to you. You thought about other women when you were making love to her and she felt it. So she lost interest in sex, *with you*. When you say, 'She is not my type' you are saying I am not *her* type. She may have found someone else. With someone who is prepared to risk all because he finds her attractive, she will come alive like a sexual tigress and respond to the risk he is taking by risking all for him.

The key is physical attraction

Rather than sexual compatibility we should see that the motor of a successful marriage is physical attraction. I would even go so far as to say that if a couple are not drawn to each other, their marriage has been functionally terminated. Physical attraction is the only aspect of our person which draws our spouse to us automatically and intuitively, without us having to act or to speak.

If a man loves his wife because she is a good person, he must always see her goodness. And she must always act compassionately if he is to love her kindness. But no mortal is capable of so much consistency and self-sacrifice. Similarly, if a woman loves her husband's personality, she will not stare at him admiringly while he is asleep since his personality sleeps too. Yet when she is attracted to him, she need do nothing at all since that animal magnetism is permanently switched on.

This does not mean to say that physical attraction is everything in marriage. This is the argument of a shallow hedonist which I strongly reject. But, it does mean that physical attraction is the beginning of every relationship, and remains a pivotal component even long after a deep love has grown. But once love has grown, our emotions dress up our beloved so that to us they always appear beautiful, even as they grow older. The magnet of the body is also what leads us to discover the metal of the personality. The culmination of every sexual experience is where the flesh peels away – thus revealing the enchantment and infinite depth of the human personality. Thus, physical attraction and love must always work in concert. Physical attraction is the bait of the relationship, whereas love is the hook. Attraction can cause you be inclined toward your spouse. But only love will sew you together as one.

I had the pleasure and privilege of discussing the film, *The Mirror Has Two Faces*, with Barbra Streisand just when she was considering making it. The central premise of the film is exactly this point: a female professor of literature falls in love with a fellow professor who loves her for her mind. But she is miserable after they marry, because he is not attracted to her body. She doesn't want him to think her intelligent, but rather beautiful. She wants to feel like a woman. She doesn't want him only to like her jokes or her insights into life. Rather, she wants to be wanted by him in her entirety, and that means finding her physically attractive, so that even when she cries or sleeps he feels drawn to her.

The power of feeling flattered

It is indeed curious how easily flattered we all are when members of the opposite sex find us physically sexy. One might have thought that being complimented for our intelligence or wit would mean so much more to us. We are, after all, human, and as a race we pride ourselves on our minds and not our bodies. And yet, a woman wants to be found sexy and attractive, and a man wants to feel irresistible. Doubtless, this can go too far. Being flattered about one's looks only is tiresome. But being flattered for being intelligent, well-educated, charming, and of resolute character isn't worth a hill of beans if it isn't couched in the assurance that one has some physical magnetism. No wife would be flattered if her husband said, 'Honey, I want you to know that I don't find you physically attractive. In fact, you're downright plain. But hell! That rocket-scientist mind of yours makes up for everything!'

The reason indeed why we are so flattered by those who love us for our looks and sex appeal, and not just our minds, speech, sense of humour, or kindness, is this: if you love someone's thoughts, speech, or actions, then in essence you love their *projections*; you are in love with their manifestations, the way in which they reveal themselves; how they behave and how they act. You love *what* they do but not *who* they are. But if you love them even without any clothes on, warts and all, even while they lie asleep naked, and in a sexual situation when they are not being articulate or even coherent, then you love them for what they are in their very essence, and not just in the way that they act.

Many would argue that I am being superficial in my argument about the importance of the attractiveness of the body. But firstly, I am not arguing that we ever overindulge the body at the expense of the soul. Rather, a husband and wife must always strive to be presentable and attractive to each other without overdoing it. The body should be a window to the soul, always pulling us toward the possibility of love with our spouse. And second, those who denigrate the body and promote the soul have a warped understanding of holiness and spirituality. The purpose of human life is to unearth the spark of God which lurks in every created thing. Our bodies are as holy as our souls, and we must always treat them with the reverence and dignity that a vessel for the divine demands.

5. Sex and traditional thought

It was partially my fault we got divorced ... I tended to place my wife under a pedestal.   Woody Allen

Bigamy is having one husband too many. Monogamy is the same.
                                    Erica Jong, *Fearless Flying*, 1974

Let me return again to the question, why indeed I, a Rabbi, am writing about sex. Being a Rabbi to young people at Oxford University and in London, relationships are the principal subject that arises in the course of counselling. And, yes, I believe fervently in marriage and the fact that dissatisfaction with physical love is a major cause of divorce. The sixties with its focus on sex as a recreational drug have left us with a disastrous legacy besides the positive achievement of liberating our discussions about sex.

But the real reason is not a pragmatic but an idealistic one. I write about sex because it is holy. It is as religious a subject as a discussion on belief in God. It is only through sexual congress that a soul is brought into this world, that a man and woman merge as one, as they were before creation, and it is one of the few mystic experiences of life in which we all share. This does not mean that it cannot be debased. Indeed, the ancient Jewish mystics were adamant that the loftier the concept, the more it was subject to abuse.

From time immemorial, however, people in general, and religious people in particular, have viewed sex as purely physical and in many cases base and degrading. And today there is a totally new, highly virulent strain of this view. Once when I was delivering a lecture in Oxford about the place of sex within society, I mentioned to the student audience what I said in the Foreword, that however petty it might sound, now that sex was so readily available, people were finding increasingly little reason to marry. Now, it can be got everywhere and at any time. So why marry?

The reaction of the students to this line of reasoning was extremely hostile. 'Imagine that', one said, 'of all the superficial, and immature reasons to marry! How shallow and desperate one must be to marry in order to have sex. How degrading.' I couldn't believe my ears. Sex! Shallow and degrading? Superficial and immature? But nearly every other student agreed with him. What if we had used other terms and had said that a man marries a woman because he really wants to get to know her, and intimacy was the only way, would they still have called this knowledge 'base and degrading.' Of course, they only dismissed the sexual commitment because to them, unlike the Bible, it involved no higher form of wisdom or enlightenment. Young people today are deprived of higher communion with the objects of their affection because to them sex is only carnal. Walking through the Tate Gallery together is what they would call a far more meaningful experience.

The ascetic fallacy

To the modern and the primitive untrained religious mind it seems only logical to postulate that the more grounded in earthly activity one becomes, and the more one indulges in sensual pleasures, the more one's spirituality decreases and the individual moves away from God. God has no body, doesn't eat or sleep, doesn't marry and certainly does not have sex, heaven forbid.

These people will argue, God does not reside on earth, but in heaven. Therefore, in order for man to come closer to God he must emulate His ways. 'The meek shall inherit the earth' and 'It is far more difficult for a rich man to enter the kingdom of heaven than it is for a camel to pass through the eye of a needle' are refrains to which we have all become accustomed. By minimising, or, better, eliminating earthly and lustful desires, man naturally comes closer to God. He must fast instead of eating, stay awake and pray and study instead of sleeping, and live a celibate life.

Hence, many religions have argued for denial of the body and a renunciation of material goods as the surest way of entering heaven. Some religions have gone so far as to advocate self-flagellation and the pursuit of a monastic life-style as further steps toward reaching heaven while on earth. Catholic clergy can't have sex and Hindus should try and minimise it. I have a Jewish friend who became a Hari Krishna. He and his wife have two children, and he swears that they have only had sex twice.

Cherishing our body

Ancient Jewish thought takes exception to all this. Far from merely allowing sex as a concession to man's primal instincts, or prescribing sex solely as the means for procreation, Judaism has argued from its inception that sex is the holiest experience and undertaking known to man. The very first verse in the Bible reads, 'In the beginning the Lord created the heavens and the earth', implying that both were equally created by God, 'and God saw all that he had made, and it was good'.

This understanding is crucial. The heavens are no more holy than the earth. It is man's obligation to find God on earth, to discover the transcendent within the immanent, and the spiritual within the physical. Human flesh is holy, and human nature is commensurately holy. We must all learn not just to forgive ourselves for being human – à la the Mediterranean man of leisure – but to revel in and celebrate our humanity. Rather than fighting our nature, we must harness it. Rather than reversing it, we must focus it. Rather than being ashamed of it, we must understand it and develop it to our advantage.

What is holy is, therefore, radically different in Judaism. All of us are conditioned to look upon the citadels of religion as being holy. A synagogue is holy as a church is holy. But in Judaism some places are holier than others, and the average Jew, for example, finds it a far greater privilege, even feels closer to heaven, praying at the Western Wall in Jerusalem than at his neighbourhood synagogue. But, similarly the bedroom can be holier than a synagogue.

In the bedroom we find and experience God through the warmth and closeness of another human being. Through the holiness of marriage, we invite God into our relationship as the spiritual partner who can elevate us above our own earthly constraints so that we can be joined together as one. If we achieve this we can be redeemed through sex.

In a moment of Jewish wit, the Talmud poignantly tells a story about Rabbinical training in which 'Rav Kahana lay hidden under the bed of Rav (his teacher) who was carousing and speaking flippantly with his wife of sexual matters; afterwards Rav had intercourse with her. Rav Kahana said to Rav: "You appear to me to be like a hungry man who has never had sex before, for you act with frivolity in your desire." Rav said to Kahana: "Are you here? Get out! It is improper for you to lie under my bed!" Kahana said to him: "This is a matter of Torah and I must study".' Indeed, the tenderness and loving affection with which a man goes about sharing exclusive intimacy with his wife is intrinsically holy.

The importance of physical matters

The outer shell therefore is, in Jewish thought, as important as inner beauty. Oscar Wilde wrote, 'It is only shallow people who do not judge by appearances. The true mystery of the world is the visible, not the invisible.' While Judaism would not go so far as that, it argues that the mystery lies in both the visible and the invisible, in the body and in the soul. According to the Talmud, for example, when the Jews were travelling through the wilderness of Sinai after their liberation from Egyptian bondage, the Almighty instructed Moses and the Jewish nation to build a tabernacle, so that He might dwell in their midst. As part of the guidelines God commanded Moses to build a brass basin for the Priests to wash their hands and feet before undertaking work in the Sanctuary.

Tradition maintains that Moses found it inappropriate that this basin was made from the daughters of Israel's brass mirrors used in Egypt by the wives. But God overruled Moses and instructed him to make the basin specifically from the mirrors since it was humble objects like these which promoted love and intimacy between husband and wife, which were most dear to Him. By the same token the Talmud says that together with the manna, the bread which God caused to rain down from heaven to sustain the Jews through their forty year sojourn in the wilderness, the Almighty rained down many different kinds of fragrances and perfumes for all the forty years as well. The great Medieval scholar Maimonides even defines a right to lingerie appropriate to sexual activity as part of the 'onah', the conjugal obligations of the husband.

Ultimately it is the body which supersedes the soul in Judaism. A Jew, for example, is not merely allowed, but obligated, to desecrate the Sabbath for the health of the body. Even though the soul will suffer, man must still compromise the sanctity of the soul for the purposes of the body. We don't exist to achieve holiness in the afterlife, we must aim for it now. And sex is essential to this. 'We attain the greatest spirituality via our physical bodies. This is the basis of Judaism, which shows us how physical pleasures are uplifted and sanctified' (Tehila Abramov).

Judaism offers guidelines, or what might be called erotic channels of communication, designed not to circumscribe our sexual routine, but to focus it and make it potent, so that sex becomes passionate and effective in conjuring up long-term emotions and commitment. It does not indulge in guilt, harping on one's sexual past or sins. On the contrary, the essence of traditional Jewish thought is *gei veiter*, always move forward. Never become mired in your past. Possessed deep within the infinite soul of man is the opportunity to reinvent himself constantly. We can always reclaim our innocence. Whatever man has done in the past, tomorrow brings a new day with limitless capacity for a new beginning.

6. Love, lust, and intimacy

I believe that it's better to be looked over than it is to be overlooked.
Mae West

Have you not as yet observed that pleasure, which is undeniably the sole motive force behind the union of the sex, is nevertheless, not enough to form a bond between them? And that, if it is preceded by desire, which impels, it is succeeded by disgust which repels? That is a law of nature which love alone can alter.
Pierre Choderols de Laclos

Like the other religions, Judaism has always had great thinkers and writers who have argued for an ascetic Judaism where sexual passion is to be limited and procreation emphasised. In April, 1996, while visiting one of Britain's leading congregations on a Sabbath morning, the Rabbi of the Synagogue launched into a diatribe against Rabbis 'who write about immodest subjects like sex and marriage. When I was young,' he continued, 'my pious Jewish grandmother would not even pronounce the word sex or even pregnancy. Rather, she spoke of a woman being 'in the family way.' Now we have Rabbis who seek to stake their reputations on it.' I quickly sunk low in my seat to avert the stares.

'What dastardly scoundrel could he have been talking about?' I
wondered aloud?

Yet ascetic thinkers are right where they emphasise modesty.
For sexual passion can only be negotiated through modesty and
respect for the other. Sex thrives specifically in a veiled arena,
where fantasy and allure are allowed their place. Moreover,
without modesty there can be no intimacy. When sex is too public
– when it is broadcast to the world – it is then no longer about two
people sharing something special and exclusive. Modesty dictates
that there is a curtain which separates my private space from the
rest of the world. Intimacy dictates that there are times when
that curtain is raised by us in order to invite in a special person
for exclusive and intimate acts.

The role of modesty

I was once approached by a 24-year-old religious Jew who had
been married for two years. The problem: he and his wife had just
had their first child, and his wife was now always tired and there
love life went from being fantastic before the birth, to dull shortly
after the birth, to non-existent from the baby's six month birthday and on. The young man said that he came to see me since he
felt he had no one within his community with whom he could
discuss these intimate issues.

I must admit that whatever pretensions to open-mindedness I
had before the meeting, they were instantly dispelled almost as
soon as he began to speak. He spoke of how his wife barely
tolerated his nightly advances and had a perpetual headache.
Why, she had now even lost the ability to climax, and this made
it impossible for him to climax as well. I was taken aback by his
immediate openness, as he described the most private details of
their intimate life. He spoke of how he had tried this position and
that position, this suggestion and that, all to no avail. He bought
her books and left them on her bed, but she just threw them out,
calling them smut. I found myself stunned into silence, and I
didn't know why.

Many secular people had sought my advice before, but never a
Chassidic Jew like myself. It bothered me that this young man
had no modesty. It bothered me that he could compromise his
wife's privacy with such abandon. Even if it was for the purpose

of enhancing their love-life, surely there was a better, a more subtle way to go about it? Moreover, everything he was saying sounded so artificial. The reason for this soon became clear. Out of a crumpled plastic bag he proceeded to pull out about ten different books on sexual technique that he had been reading of late. Everything from the *Kama Sutra* to *Secrets of How To Please a Woman in Bed*.

'What are you doing with all this stuff?' I asked him incredulously.

'What do you mean, what am I doing? I'm doing whatever it takes to make our sex life more exciting and save our marriage. Haven't you listened to anything I've been saying?' 'I've tried all this stuff with my wife, but she is just so inhibited. Every time we try something new, she complains it hurts her too much, or she's not in the mood, or she's just tired and wants to go to sleep. Sometimes I wish she would just take the baby and move into her parents' place and leave me alone.'

After some further enquiries, it soon emerged that the reason his wife seemed so tired in the months following the baby's birth was that her husband, the sex guru, had not lifted a finger to help her with all her new-found chores, and she simply couldn't cope. She felt neglected and unloved and she responded by subconsciously turning off in the bedroom. However good his intentions, this young man was wrecking the life of his spouse and endangering their marriage not because of any problem with a prudish wife, but rather because he wanted to be a husband only in the bedroom. Theirs was a crisis of intimacy, not of sex or lust.

Ever since the publication of *The Joy of Sex* by Dr Alex Comfort in 1971, we have been flooded with amazing guide books each purporting to give us the kind of sexual and sensual pleasure that will have us careering through the ceiling's rafters on the way to the moon, or your money back. It seems odd, however, that none should offer techniques specifically designed to maximise human emotional intimacy. The books in question can teach us which sexual positions are most enjoyable, but they do not similarly emphasise which are the most conducive to a shared and loving experience whose after-effects will not dissipate with sexual climax. Have you ever wondered about the startling fact that even if we watched a couple in the throws of passion, having the most exciting sexual encounter, we still wouldn't even know necessarily if they love each other?

Don't fall into the trap of equating love and lust

Whereas love is about wanting to draw closer to someone, lust is about wanting to possess someone. Whereas love is about wanting to hold someone, lust is about wanting to use someone. Whereas love deepens with time, lust is extinguished with time. Whereas love deepens with every encounter, lust is extinguished with even a single encounter. Love is about sharing, while lust is about taking. Love treats the other like a person, lust like an object. With love you try and win the other. With lust you try and possess the other. Love is about mutual surrender, while lust involves a winner and a loser. The objective therefore is to use sex to generate commitment, not to smother or repress it. Lust leads to sex, and sex leads to love, and love leads to further commitment – and we should not impede that which comes naturally and is healthy. Notice that the ten commandments prohibit a man from lusting after his neighbour's wife. The fact that the Bible specified one's neighbour's wife directly implies that it is perfectly acceptable to lust after your own wife. Otherwise, the verse could simply have said that it is forbidden to lust after any woman. But lust must be treated as the means to the ends of love.

As I said above, in ancient Jewish thought sexual congress is a metaphor for God's creation of, and interaction with, His world. Sex is said to bring about the celestial unity of masculine and feminine energies. God Himself is said to have masculine and feminine aspects that express themselves as His immanence in history and His transcendence in creation. There is God's finite and limiting energy representing form, and the infinite and unbounded energy of God the Creator, representing substance. The masculine God of history, who intervenes in the ways of the world and fills the world with His light is represented by a line. The infinite God of Creation is represented by a circle, an energy that hovers above the cosmos, sustaining and animating the Universe constantly. When the circle and the line are joined together there is a burst and creation of life.

Lest we believe that there are two gods, two distinct energies, a Creator of men and a separate Creator of women – that the God of history is not the same as the God of creation – the fact that the two genders unite in sexual congress shows that really God is one and that both male and female emanate from different aspects of the same God. Thus, sex in a literal, but also in a cosmological sense, demonstrates the underlying unity of creation. It is for this reason that Judaism has always identified sex as the most holy of all human endeavours. Since our world was created as an arena to demonstrate the unity of God, no other act demonstrates this better than the physical union of male and female, strangers who become lovers, and lovers who are also friends.

Part Two

Sexual Techniques: the Mechanics of Sex

1. Can men and women really enjoy sex together?

Marriage is the price men pay for sex; sex is the price women pay for marriage.   Anonymous

After fifteen years of marriage, they finally achieved sexual compatibility. They both had a headache.   Anonymous

My wife doesn't. Understand me?   Anonymous

I once asked a gynaecologist in Oxford who would sometimes attend my lectures whether he agreed that loss of passion was the greatest impediment to marital bliss. He responded with an emphatic, 'No'. 'The greatest problem with sex is that men are so impatient.' They just want to get on with the business, irrespective whether the woman is ready. You should see the women who come to me for treatment, Shmuley, with torn tissue because men want to have sex with them before they are even prepared. They don't care if the women are enjoying it, or even if they're in pain. I'd say this is the most common problem I deal with, especially for single women.'

Gender differences

Nonetheless, in spite of this clear difference in sexual temperament, up until the publication and phenomenal success of *Men are From Mars, Women are From Venus*, it was almost impossible for anyone to make any mention of gender differences between men and women without being clobbered for it. Since then, an avalanche of studies has spelled out just how different men and women are in day to day life, and libraries of books have been published on different male and female expectations of dating, relationships, and marriage and love. It might even be said that the whole science of male/female relationships today revolves around trying to find harmony and build a bridge across the natural, biological divide.

Surprisingly, however, how incredibly different men and women are sexually still receives little attention. Specifically, the greatest male/female problem of all, namely, the difficulty they have in achieving mutual satisfaction together, when that satisfaction is achieved in such radically different ways, is ignored. This is the more surprising since these differences are so obvious. Men always complain of women who 'just lie there' and don't participate sufficiently in the sexual act, while women, especially wives, complain of men who just want 'quickies' and do not focus on wooing their wives into sex. This accounts for the disappointing sexual routine of most married couples. A recent study showed that although married couples have sex twice a week on average, the average length of each sexual encounter is thirteen minutes (most readers are now saying, 'Really, that long!').

The consequences of these sexual differences are staggering. According to *Sex in America*, the most comprehensive and methodologically sound survey of Americans' sexual practices ever conducted, it is women who experience far greater problems of sexual satisfaction and interest than men. While only 16 per cent of men lacked interest in sex, an astonishing 35 per cent of women regularly have no interest. And while only 7 per cent of men are unable to orgasm during sex, a sizable 34 per cent of women have a chronic difficulty. Only 3 per cent of men experience pain during sex, while 15 per cent of women complain of ongoing sexual discomfort. In addition, 19 per cent of women experience problems with lubrication. By contrast, the only sexual problems which men generally experience are anxiety about performance (15 per cent), and the problem of premature ejaculation (29 per cent).

Patient sex

But all of these problems in sexual relations pale in significance with regard to the simple fact that men seem interested in sex, while women want romance and love. For women foreplay is a glorious part of the act. A recent statistic shows that 79 per cent of women enjoy the caressing and hugging involved in foreplay far more than sex itself, whereas 83 per cent of men see foreplay as nothing but the prelude to sex. For them romance is a road which leads to sex, and who wants to waste time on the road?

How then did the Creator expect men and women to enjoy sex together when they have such different sexual metabolisms? Men must exert considerable control to slow themselves down if they are to achieve the same pace as the woman they are with. And, in fact, the lack of sexual passion in marriage, which has come to be the leading contemporary cause of divorce, is directly attributable to men who don't take the time to romance the women they are with. This seems a colossal biological imperfection in humans and doesn't match the easy harmony found in the animal kingdom.

The only answer to this question is that God intended us to practice sex where the focus is not on pleasure, *but on the achievement of unity and symmetry between man and woman*. Where the interests and the focus on the body fade and where the personality becomes highlighted and pronounced. God requires from us a situation where a husband is not interested in ejaculation and climax so much as in finding a shared rhythm in sex with his wife. Human sex, therefore, necessitates a focus on harmony and intimacy rather than mere pleasure or reproduction.

Sex, a hot line to your wife

In order for the sexual act between men and women to be fully pleasurable and fulfilling for both participants, a man cannot just climb on his wife in some disguised form of autoeroticism. He must ensure that the crest of their sexual wave is arched in a manner where his wife can join him on its peak. He must have a genuine concern for his wife's complete participation in the sexual act. And if he rushes things, he will end up the loser, because she will lose her interest and no husband will be excited by a wife who is bored of sex with him or who is insufficiently stimulated and is thus a lesser participant in the act.

To be in harmony, we must see sex as an exalted form of communication where the participants are constantly gauging each other's rate of response. Sex must become a form of knowledge as in the Bible, which has no word for sex apart from 'knowledge': 'And Adam came to know his wife Eve.' For animals sex is no more than impregnation, as they have no dysfunction in sexual harmony. But humans are different. They can show someone patience as a sign that we cherish our sexual partner and want to get to know him or her better; that we understand that they comprise not just a delectable body, but also an attractive personality. And when a husband slows down in sex and focuses intensely on his wife's beauty, her interest, and especially her response, he does just that. It means that he is not just rushing on to her, that he is not being selfish and that he is taking time for her instead of merely masturbating on her.

The downward spiral toward adultery

This sexual harmony which is so deeply satisfying to both husbands and wives, when it is achieved, will help prevent the terrible downward spiral of infidelity which affects all too many contemporary marriages. Since a man's libido seems to thrive on horizontal rather than vertical renewal, what most men want in sex is new flesh and new partners. They are not naturally monogamous, and they quickly tire of the same body in sex. Women, however, thrive on vertical renewal. They do not seek new bodies, so much as deeper and more loving expressions occurring within the same relationship. They want to try many new things and explore different methods of communication with the same man.

This gender difference leads to a downward spiral in many marriages that goes something like this. A couple marries after falling in love. Their first year together is filled with romance and excitement. They pleasure each other physically, go out a lot, and seem entirely focused on each other. By the second year this slows down somewhat, and by the third year they have entered a predictable cycle of work and keeping up with the frenetic activity of modern life. They raise the kids and take out the rubbish. They don't have as much time for each other, and the spark begins to be lost from their marriage.

But being a man, the husband's eyes begins to wander. It is not that he cheats. Rather, he is not nearly as focused on his wife as he once was. She feels this and begins to resent it. Her irritation builds as she notices the inordinate attention he begins to pay other women, and how he admires their beauty and body parts. She dresses up for him, but this only partly addresses the problem. His mind still seems focused elsewhere. Even when he is here, he is not fully here. He does not even listen to her fully when she speaks. She becomes resentful. The more distracted he seems, the more hostile she becomes.

As part of her self-defense mechanism, she lashes out at him more and more, and becomes critical of his actions. She begins to find fault with everything he does. He begins to shout at her that she makes him feel like he can't do anything right. Everything he does, she finds unworthy. He becomes consumed with self-pity, and convinces himself that he deserves some warmth. He begins to speak more to the woman across from his desk in the office whom he has always found attractive anyway.

His guilt is mitigated by the fact that he dismisses his wife as uncaring. The other woman is very complimentary to him. He starts paying her a lot of attention. She catches him staring at her frequently, and conversely she is always telling him how wonderful he is. Soon, he thinks to himself, 'Why is my wife not this nice to me? Why does this stranger think I'm special, but my own wife treats me with such derision?' Rather than think to himself that his lack of affection and attention toward his wife has caused her to express her pain through antagonism and bitterness, he instead faults his wife as a cold, selfish, and unconcerned woman.

A couple's conjugal duties

This process must be nipped in the bud by both couples, though the problem lies mainly with men. Many husbands think that they can ignore their wives outside the bedroom, and yet expect them to perform within the bedroom. This doesn't work. A wife who isn't romanced during the day is not going to feel loving at night. Often, she will even resist her husband's advances, and refuse to allow him to touch her. But, when a man and a woman have a very healthy sex life, and when they seek to bring harmony to their vastly differing libidos, they ensure that they do not need to find sexual satisfaction outside the marriage.

The reason for this blind spot of husbands is not hard to find. Throughout recent and less recent history sex has always been treated as a man's right and a woman's duty. Whether or not

women enjoyed sex was immaterial. They existed for the man's
pleasure and women were seen as immoral if they enjoyed themselves. Modern sex-experts have only recently discovered the
female sexual nature, and prior to the eighteenth century the
female orgasm remained an undiscovered mystery. Even medical
experts like Dr William Acton still wrote in 1857 concerning a
female patient, 'She assured me that she felt no sexual passions
whatever. Her passion for her husband was of a platonic kind,
and far from wishing to stimulate his frigid feelings, she doubted
whether it would be right or not.'

Sexual desire in the Bible

Yet, for those who know the Bible female sexual desire is nothing
new. Whereas feminist authors are only beginning to assert the
strong sexual nature of women, the Talmud actually declared
2000 years ago that a woman's sexual passion is far greater than
that of a man. Indeed, Nachmanides (1194-1270), one of the
greatest Jewish scholars, explains in his commentary on the
Bible that when God declared that Eve would long for Adam after
eating from the tree of knowledge, 'craving (teshukah) represents
an exceedingly great sexual desire for her husband.'

Feminists moreover, portray religion as encouraging women to
subdue any trace of sexual longing. But the Bible conceives of sex
within marriage as the woman's right and the man's duty. Far
from denying the sexual component of female desire, the Torah
actually obligates a man to pleasure his wife to the point where
she reaches sexual climax before him. For a man to have sex with
his wife without affording her pleasure is an abuse. The Rabbis
wrote about sex that the 'mitzvah of onah' (conjugal relations) is
regarded as both a need and a pleasure especially of women
('baalei hanefesh, shaar hakedusha'). Sex is not a luxury of
marriage but its most basic necessity. Just as a desire for food
connects our bodies with our souls, we have to want each other
sexually to make husband and wife one.

Under Jewish law a wife's contentment is the key to sexual
harmony as sex is the most central element of marriage. The
Bible, in fact, records three fundamental unqualified rights
which a woman possesses in marriage: food, clothing/shelter, and
conjugal rights. But only if either husband or wife withholds sex

from the other over a period of time, are they immediately dubbed to be a 'mored', or 'moredes', a 'rebellious spouse'. A Jewish court would grant the aggrieved party an immediate divorce.

'This is because onah [the sexual rights]' the Rabbis explain, 'is the essence of marriage and to withhold romance and sex from a spouse is to cause them physical pain. Food and clothing can be handled in court, but a withdrawal from "onah" is a functional termination of married life.' The man's conjugal duties to his wife are not there to provide marital relations. They must be pleasurable to the woman, for without pleasure, the Rabbis explain, there is no bonding. It is for this reason that that Iggeret Hakodesh, a fourteenth-century 'letter' written from a pious sage to his son on the occasion of his marriage, encourages a man to exert every effort to pleasure his wife:

> You should begin with words that will draw her heart to you and will settle her mind and make her happy ...
>
> Tell her things which will produce in her desire, attachment, love, willingness, and passion ...
>
> Win her heart with words of charm and seduction ...
>
> Never have sex with your wife while she is sleepy, for your minds will not be unified ...
>
> Never hasten to arouse her desire ...
>
> Begin in a pleasing manner of love, so that she will achieve satisfaction before you.

We can still learn from this. For one of the things that has most undermined sex in the modern age is the complete focus on the body, to the exclusion of everything else. In areas of the flesh, men and women are indeed different and cannot achieve harmony, but in areas of the personality and the soul, they can become one. This is why pleasure is so central, because enjoyment and passion elicit our total character and call forth our complete participation. It is capable of turning into the deepest form of knowledge, becoming an experience which lifts both participants up: the body peels away, masks begin to fade, and what is left is a vulnerable and feeling human being.

2. Is there a kosher *Kama Sutra*?

If the psyche is unwilling, no amount of technique can persuade it;
and if the psyche is willing, no lack of technique can dissuade it.
Ann Aldrich

There's no norm in sex. Norm is the name of a guy who lives in
Brooklyn.   Dr Alex Comfort

Katie and Peter were married for seven years. They had a deep
love for each other, but both felt that the fire had gone from their
marriage. Previously, they never tried anything too kinky in their
sex lives, because there was no need for it. They both felt extremely satisfied. But now they decided to experiment with every
new sexual position, in the car, in the kitchen. He even bought a
motorbike so they could try it on that. Surely novelty and experimentation would do the trick, Peter thought.

And it worked. But only for Peter. He found new life by
instigating new sexual techniques in their marriage. But Katie
felt that while things were more exciting, they were no longer as
close. Peter became frustrated with his wife's preference for
missionary-position sex. 'My husband thinks I'm a prude, but
there is something beautiful in making love while looking into
your husband's eyes. I want to see how much he is enjoying me.'

Spicy sex

There can be no doubt. Sexual experimentation, such as Peter's
in this example, has received bucket-loads of attention over the
past few decades. The *Kama Sutra*, with its hundreds of sexual
positions, has once again become a classic, and most sexual
partners see the myriad position possibilities as a means by
which to bring newness and experimentation into lovemaking,
rather than pursue the same old sexual routine. Most people are
convinced, however, that religion, being totally prudish about
sex, would of course insist on the missionary position rather than
on something really kinky and exciting such as, say, penetration
from behind.

But, I agree. Couples should leave no stone unturned in their sexual repertoire, always renewing the spontaneity and freshness of their relationship. The rule of thumb is that anything that enhances the love, excitement, and intimacy of a marriage, while not compromising its sanctity or modesty, is always a good thing. Seen from this perspective, the *Kama Sutra* – its explicit nature aside – can be a kosher book.

In this respect, Peter, in the story above, was absolutely justified in trying every new thing to bring excitement back into his marriage. Judaism, however, while agreeing with his enthusiasm also insists that amidst the various experimental sexual positions there should be one principal position, and that of course is the much-maligned but still much-practiced missionary position. In this respect, it was Katie who was right.

Total unity

Jewish sexual laws revolve around a constant attempt to promote and sustain emotional intimacy of married couples through physical intimacy. And we can immediately and intuitively appreciate how the missionary position leads to this closeness and familiarity. In no other sexual position do we see a meeting of the mouths accompanied by a full integration of all the limbs. Not only are husband and wife locked together in the genital region, but they coalesce in their totality so that even in appearance they become as one. The missionary position allows us to experience something which is quintessentially human.

To support this point about total unity the ancient Rabbis, for example, draw our attention to the fact that humans are the only creatures who make love facing each other. And in fact, biologists have suggested that the size of the human penis – which, percentage-wise is far larger than that of most mammals – is to enable humans to have sexual intercourse in a face-to-face position (and who said size doesn't matter?). The Zohar, the most important work of the Cabalah, Jewish mysticism, adds to this that every person has three essential components, body, spirit, and soul. The body is our husk ('klipah'), the spirit is our life-force, and the soul is the spark of God serving as an umbilical chord connecting us to the divine, and the missionary position unites a husband and wife on all three levels. In the missionary position, a couple can kiss and exchange the breath of life ('ruchos'). They can whisper in each others' ear, and thereby unite their spirits ('nefashos'), and they can hold one another, their bodies ('gufim') becoming one flesh.

In the missionary position we can converse and utter meaningful whispers of affection which would otherwise be closed off to us. As we hug and embrace we hold onto each other's backs, thereby demonstrating that we love and accept every part of our lover's being. We cherish not only their more distinctive and sublime features, like their intelligence and facial beauty, but even something as humble and non-distinct as their back. (And women have overwhelmingly stated in study after study that what they enjoy most in sex is this physical embrace.) Other sexual positions, while pleasurable in their own right, can only close off outlets for some or all other types of union: verbal, mental, or even emotional.

And ultimately there is nothing more sexy, more seductive, or more alluring than to watch our husband or wife come alive as a sexual being, suspending their conscious processes and allowing themselves to drift into an ethereal world of sexual pleasure and excitement, responding to the activities that we have initiated. Through our direct eye-to-eye contact we feel and discover the essence and beauty of our partners. All of us hate being stared at, and in everyday social situations we avoid direct eye-to-eye contact as much as possible. The essence of the person is in their eyes. There is too much truth in our eyes and we feel naked and unmasked. But in our spouse's eyes we peer deep into their irreducible essence. It affords us the ultimate act of truth, openness and knowledge.

Complete surrender

What the missionary position affords us is a physical means by which total surrender can be achieved. When I was a kid in school we would test whether or not our friends really trusted us by asking them to fall backward while we stood behind to catch them. If they were prepared to fall all the way, then they trusted us. But if they would move a foot at the last minute and catch themselves, then we felt like we were not trusted. Relationships too require a metaphorical 'fall' in order to ascertain trust. It involves total, as opposed to incremental, surrender.

If you love someone then you are prepared to fall into their arms without any reservations or safety-nets, because the underlying premise of your love is your confidence that they will never hurt you and will only do what is truly in your interest and to your benefit. And what is absolutely indispensable to complete surrender is trust, for those whom we love most are also those whom we most trust.

Consequently, lack of trust is what I believe to be one of the major causes of the deterioration and breakdown of marriage in the twentieth century. Marriage today is not about total surrender so much as focused submission. We abdicate part or parts of ourselves rather than all of ourselves. Modern society revolves so strongly around independence and self-reliance that we never seem to depend entirely upon even our husbands and wives.

We therefore do not deliver ourselves over to one another sufficiently. Marriage is no longer an act of complete capitulation, but rather incremental acquiescence. We are prepared to offer into the marriage those aspects of ourselves and our lives which we would agree are integral to the endeavour, but never any more. But, the problem with this focused surrender is that, since neither party is willing to let go completely, you never become one unit in the way which you might if you were more believing.

Other sexual positions are flawed like this partial surrender in that they principally bring together genital and other erogenous zone but never a complete orchestration of the entire body. The lovers have connected, but only on one plane. They have had sex, but they have not made love. They have only surrendered a region of their bodies, a geographical part of themselves, or a single dimension of their personalities. They have had a great time, but each at different times and at different moments. Rates of breathing and verbal utterances, the digging of nails and the clawing of flesh can all serve as a gauge of our partner's state of arousal, but these are no substitute for looking into their eyes. In the same way that one discerns whether or not one's associate is listening to one's words by studying their eyes, one measures the delights felt by one's spouse during intimacy. As our husband or wife's eyes roll back in ecstasy, we are transported with them to a realm where the soul transcends the body and the human form dominates earthly matter.

3. Your spouse: a friend or a lover?

Platonic friendship – the interval between the introduction and
the first kiss.
                                                        Sophie Irene Loeb

I have always detested the belief that sex is the chief bond between
man and woman. Friendship is far more human.
                                                        Agnes Smedley

Love is a matter of chemistry. Sex is physics   Anonymous

Husbands are chiefly good lovers when they are betraying their
wives.
                                                        Marilyn Monroe

One of the rules of dating is that when a man tires of the woman
he is seeing (or in many cases when a woman tires of a man), he
cannot simply call her up and end it. No, that would be too
heartless and cruel. Rather, dumping her comes in the form of the
famous Let's-be-friends phone call. 'I really like you,' he tells her.
'But I like you as a friend. I love you more like a sister.' Or, 'I
really like you, but the lab results have just returned and I only
have four weeks to live, and I'd like to spend it with my pets.' Or,
'I'm crazy about you. But I've decided that I'm just not good
enough for you. So, I've found a new woman in my life who is far
less perfect.' I even know a man who told a girlfriend he wanted
to ditch, that he had just discovered that he was gay and had
fallen in love with his best friend. Excuses aside, everyone is
supposed to understand that lovers cannot also be friends. Yet,
amazingly, when it comes to marriage people believe that entirely
different rules apply.

Friends in marriage

In my years of counseling couples, I have encountered two kinds
of marriages. There are those couples who trust each other im-
plicitly and explicitly. They are each other's confidants and most
trusted companions. They share every secret and they depend
and rely on each other utterly. No wedge can be driven between
them because they are inseparable. They have friends outside the
marriage, but they relate to their friends as a single unit, as a

couple. They are therefore more friendly with couples than they are with individual men and women. Communication is the norm in such marriages, not lovemaking. Their union is based far more on compatibility – similar interests – than on raw physical attraction.

These couples lack no intimacy in their life. So what's their problem?

There is little or no passion. They have great conversations, but when they undress in the bedroom the newspaper comes out and the television is immediately switched on. Theirs is a love like water, not like fire. Based on trust and intimacy, their whole relationship is more about compatibility than attraction. It is not a passionate relationship and this has both positive and negative aspects. Positive because it means there is deep trust and they rarely argue. Why would they fight? They have no fire. They do not make each other's blood boil. But since there is no flame, their marriage is predictable.

Lovers in marriage

Then there are the husbands and wives who are lovers. Theirs is a passionate, fiery union. They fight and argue constantly. They do not, however, completely love or even trust each other. When they need advice about important life-decisions, they do not seek it from each other. There is little calm in their marriage, and it is almost always tempest-tossed. But one thing they have is plenty of fire. They have a great intensity of emotion toward one other.

They are constantly arguing and making up, with great passion and fervour. Their lovemaking sessions are wonderful. But they can't seem to get along and truly communicate outside the bedroom. They have physical knowledge, but not emotional intimacy. The wife has her friends, and the husband has his. They don't really do things as a couple, and when they do, it is for a specific reason. They love each other, but they don't necessarily like each other. They don't share similar tastes and they are not similar types. Their marriage is a constant crescendo of highs and lows. For this reason they love each other passionately, but they also get on one another's nerves. There is nothing dull about their marriage, but then there is nothing serene about it either. Like a guitar, their strings are strung too tightly.

How we achieve both

Yet, the problem inherent in this paradox is that for any marriage to be a success, it must somehow bridge this gap and fuse together conflicting opposites. A marriage requires both fire and water in order to be a success. Any truly successful marriage must perforce synthesize the contradictory ingredients of passion and intimacy. We do indeed want our spouse to be both our lover, but also our best friend. Any truly successful marriage must perforce synthesise the contradictory ingredients of both passion and intimacy. And this is what kosher sex is all about. For kosher sex is passionate lovemaking which leads to intimacy. There are moments in our life where we want novelty, romance, passion, and excitement. We want our spouse to whisk us to Kathmandu for a romantic weekend. We want to jump from hotel to hotel, ripping each other's clothes off, laughing giddily together as we stroll down the Champs Elysée hand in hand. But there is another side to marriage as well.

After a couple of weeks of hotels and living on airplanes, we want to come home to the serenity, comfort and predictability of our own home. At least half of a life we wish not for novelty but for sameness. We want a marriage where we can talk and exchange thoughts. We want companionship and friendship. We wish to share our life with a spouse who not only makes us career through the rafters of the ceiling, but grow intellectually and emotionally, someone with whom we can not only rush to the bedroom with, but with whom we can build an entire home. In short, we desire calmness amidst the frequent storms.

No marriage is truly successful or fulfilling unless both these opposites are accommodated. But fire and water cancel each other out. So how can we achieve both simultaneously?

Joining fiery and watery love

Recognising this dilemma, the Bible, more than three millennia ago, ingeniously offered the following solution. Every month, there must be two weeks devoted to physical love, and two weeks devoted to intellectual communication and emotional intimacy. And what better cycle to follow then the exact rhythm of the female body itself. While husband and wife are permitted to each other and indulge in sex for two weeks they will forge deep emotional bonds. They unite physically and feel close emotionally. Their passionate physical life deepens their emotion and feeling for one another.

When the woman's menses begin, their two weeks are up – just before monotony sets in. They must separate for the five days of menstruation and for seven days thereafter and maintain a strict period of sexual abstinence. During this period they will be able to capitalise on everything which has been achieved in their physical union, transmuting the relationship onto a deeper emotional and intellectual plane. They develop the friendship side of their marriage and they focus on discovering the personality rather than the flesh.

Feeding off each other's minds rather than bodies, they talk instead of caress, share secrets instead of kiss, and discuss one another's work-day. Focusing on the broader aspects of their life outside of the bedroom, they can discuss the children, their plans for a family holiday, their business relationships and their relationship with their respective parents. It is a rhythm which is healthy for the woman and accords with the natural impulses which accompany menstruation. Many women have an innate aversion to sex during menstruation. A period of abstention allows the walls of the uterus to rebuild itself and affords a woman an opportunity of not having to accommodate her husband sexually at a time of physical discomfort.

As the days pass by and they begin to hunger for each other, they don't immediately follow their instincts and grab for each other. Rather, they allow their non-physical communication to build up into an intense longing for each other. Their libidinous reserve replenishes itself until, twelve days after they have separated, their love for one another reaches its crescendo, when their inner fire and passion for each other that has been escalating leaps out like the eruption of a volcano, and they unite together in fiery physical bliss. Like the time when they first married, they enjoy a monthly honeymoon in which they discover each other's bodies as if for the first time.

Symbolising this imminent rebirth, on the night of their reunion with their husbands, orthodox Jewish women go to a 'mikveh,' a small ritual pool of water, where they immerse themselves after the twelve day separation of their period. Emerging from the water pool is a symbol of physical regeneration and spiritual renewal, which leads a woman back to her husband like a bride to groom, reminding them of the enormous passion they experienced when they first discovered the pleasures of the flesh. It is a totally private affair. No one present, save for a female mikveh attendant, which reflects the beautiful feminine mystique and hidden charms of sexual eroticism.

Marriage is meant to be exciting

Couples who truly wish to become lovers but also best friends must develop these two antithetical dimensions of their marriage. Anything else is a recipe for regularity which snuffs out the excitement of marriage. People are living, animated creatures. If we were only cerebral, our lives would be fairly predicable. But we are emotional beings, and therefore hate routine, which ultimately bores us. Too many couples try to make their marriages proceed along a straight line. They share a bed constantly, and wonder why their sex life loses its spark after a short while. They have sex several times a week, with no break, and wonder why it comes in short, forgettable spasms. In truth, people cannot proceed straight, but rather must tack like a sailboat between passion and intimacy.

This marriage pattern also helps in attaining harmony between the male and female libido. As mentioned earlier, male sexual desire thrives on novelty and newness. Men have a very short sexual attention span, and quickly tire of an available body that provides no adventure and which can be conquered without a chase. The period of sexual abstention, therefore, provides a constant challenge whereby a husband lusts and hungers for his unavailable wife, rather than chasing after his forbidden secretary. He will never tire of his wife's body, because for two weeks of each month flesh remains outside his grasp, ever elusive, beckoning him for more. And when his wife finally becomes available, he makes passionate love to her for two weeks until he is indeed satiated, and does not feel like he needs any other body. And so the cycle repeats itself.

4. Is oral sex wrong?

The 1950s were ten years of foreplay.　　　　Germaine Greer

Sex is not some sort of pristine, reverent ritual. You want reverence and pristine, go to church.　　　　Cynthia Heimel

We are all sexual creatures, and to try and stifle our innate sexuality is mistaken at best, and hazardous at worst. It was Sigmund Freud who first warned us of the dangers of repressing our sexual nature. Likewise, in the Cabalah, the Jewish esoteric disciplines, the emotions are compared to flowers which are planted by the gardener, representing the intellect. An emotion which grows without guidance, without a gardener, is a weed. It is an unseemly and destructive emotion. And the trick is to have our mind channel and direct emotions, instead of suppressing them, so that they attach us to right things and repel us from the wrong things.

Channeling sexual energy

In marriage this is equally true. It is perhaps more difficult because we have to tend to it together, but a couple must always try and accommodate each other's sexual needs, even if at times this may seem distasteful. To make their marriage work, their sexual energy requires guidance and focus. They have to try and find sexual harmony. But there can be no doubt that this may be hard to bring about.

I once received a surprise call from a very religious Jew, Joseph, who asked if he could come up from the south of England to discuss a personal problem. He was twenty three years old and had recently married a girl his age who was also very religious. He arrived without his wife, and we met in my living room where he closed all the doors and the windows, making sure that no one could listen. 'I need your help. Being religious I have, of course, remained a virgin until I married, and so I have a lot of pent-up sexual energy. I want to try everything, but my wife feels disgusted with some of the things I suggested. When I asked her for oral sex, she started to cry and accused me of degrading her. Does she prefer that I fantasise about doing it with strangers? I may be religious, but I'm also a man.'

Can a husband and wife who entertain vastly different ideas about sex, as in the story above, still love each other and find great happiness? Many religious people feel an innate sense of discomfort with any sexual practice that is not strictly missionary-position sex, or what they refer to as 'natural'. They are mistakenly of the opinion that sex is only for procreation and that it is a sin to derive pleasure from sex. This question is especially important in an age in which so many non-religious husbands and wives erroneously attribute the problems in their marriage to sexual incompatibility.

Sexual focus

What both sides forget is that shared pleasure in sex is the corner-stone of marriage. As I said above, when practiced with sanctity, love, and commitment, far from being an animalistic act, sex is humankind's loftiest pursuit where a man and a woman, freed from all inhibition, can capture the other's essence. The core Jewish teaching on marital sex is, for example, that a fulfilling sex life is essential to a healthy marriage and prudishness has no place between two committed adults. And indeed, all marital surveys show that of all the ingredients that lead to a happy marriage, a healthy and satisfying sex life is foremost among them.

In Judaism, the Rabbis specifically point out that the human female is the only species in existence who can cohabit when she is pregnant, thus demonstrating conclusively that for humans sex is not just about procreation. And the Zohar adds beautifully that the Sabbath candles are a symbol of a wife's ability to rekindle her husband's lust and passion for her. Just as the Shabbos candles flicker with a great intensity and burning, always renewing themselves after a flicker and a momentary dimming of the flames, so too a woman can always renew her husband's interest in her even after a hiatus of passion and excitement.

God wishes for husbands and wives to be truly happy together. 'Had sexual relations been only physical,' the medieval rabbi

Menachem Meiri argued, 'the Bible would not have referred to them as yediah [knowledge].' But this cannot be achieved by throwing in more and more sexual prohibitions that limits a couple's sexual repertoire beyond the already very difficult constraints of strict monogamy. To add an unnecessary prudishness is to sometimes invite disaster in marriage and inhibit a couple's bonding process. Total sexual focus on our spouse is the ultimate form of holy sex. The great Biblical commentator Rashi writes that the true connection between husband and wife cannot be achieved without pleasure: 'since if she does not enjoy intimacy she will not cleave to him'. And this type of integral and mutually satisfying bond is specifically achieved with pleasure as the central ingredient in the sexual adhesive.

Asceticism

Nonetheless, some religious people may counter that pleasure may be the central ingredient of marriage, but that this may only be achieved through the missionary position. In Judaism, for example, many students of Jewish thought will cite the Code of Jewish law which advises husbands and wives to minimise direct oral contact of the genitals; or the rulings in the Code of Jewish Law which says that for a man to kiss his wife in the genital region is lewd, thereby prohibiting cunnilingus, and that wasted seed is a severe prohibition, thereby prohibiting oral sex on a man.

But to see these pronouncements as laws is simply a travesty of the truth. In Judaism the more conservative sexual rulings are given only as advice. This can easily be proven. The great Medieval Jewish codifier Maimonides who, while advising husbands and wives to abstain from an over-indulgence in non-missionary sex, still writes that the actual law is: 'A man's wife is permitted to him and therefore, whatever he and his wife wish to pursue sexually, they may do. They may have intercourse whenever it pleases them and he may kiss any organ he wishes, and he may have intercourse in a natural or unnatural manner.'

The Rabbis did not say that a man should not look at his wife's genitals, but rather that he should not *stare*, because all too many men degrade a woman by reducing her to a small number of erogenous zones to the detriment of the total personality. We

should be concerned above all else with holistic matrimonial
unity rather than a base obsession with lower bodily parts in
which no man or woman is distinguished as individuals. Staring
at genitals leads to erotic parts of the body losing their mystique
and becoming as unexciting as an elbow. But there will be times
when seeing your partner's body is essential to erotic arousal, and
the Rabbis never intended to mechanise sex to the point where
spontaneity is snuffed out.

Similarly oral sex. While it is true that willful destruction of
seed is a severe Biblical prohibition, known as onanism, this
applies in cases where husbands go out of their way to avoid
insemination and destroy seed – as in the case of coitus interrup-
tus, where withdrawal actually lessens pleasure and is only done
to ensure that one's wife does not become pregnant. The Biblical
prohibition is, in fact, mentioned where Onan withdrew from his
sister-in-law Tamar because he refused to have a child that would
be named after his dead brother. It is truly unnatural because
withdrawal and the spilling of seed involves a total cessation of
sexual pleasure for both husband and wife, which is only practiced in contempt of the impregnation process. But in oral sex the
purpose is not to destroy seed. Rather it is to try something new
and pleasurable, something which will cause husband and wife
to increase their dependency on each other, and lessen their
dependency on strangers. To repeat: Judaism opposes the willful
destruction of seed, but not sexual practices which may sometimes involve the *spilling* of seed, but which are pursued for
purposes of pleasuring husband and wife.

There have indeed been Jewish thinkers who have pursued a
very ascetic line with regards to sex. They felt it was primarily
about procreation and that man must not indulge in sex but
rather harness and cultivate his 'higher' faculties, like his mind
and his intelligence. But this asceticism in Judaism is nothing
more than an individual commentator's personal taste and advice. The great medieval Jewish legalist, Maimonides wrote that
'a man's wife was permitted to him, and that he might do whatever he wishes to do with his wife he may do – he may have
intercourse whenever he pleases and he may kiss any organ he
wishes, and he may have intercourse in a natural or unnatural
manner.' Yet, later he suggests that he refrain from these
practices because sex was for procreation, a notion which Nach-

manides traces back to the 'impure Greeks'. But everyone agrees that Maimonidean asceticism is *not* the law, but rather personal advice from an individual. For a Jew sex is holy so long as it is always designed to increase the mutual dependency and intimacy of husband and wife.

Sexual repression through religion

Every so often we are scandalized when we read of very religious people having cavorted with prostitutes or cheating on their spouse. We read all too often of members of the clergy being accused of child sexual abuse, or found with child pornographic materials. (Moreover, statistics show that among the very religious one-third have had extramarital affairs, and three-quarters have had premarital sexual experiences, *The Janus Report on Sexual Behavior*.)

I have the greatest pity for religious individuals who make these terrible errors, because most of the time they are indeed devout and pious. But they themselves suppressed, or are being asked to repress, the strongest aspects of human nature. This is simply impossible. If we heard of monks who took vows of starvation, where they were not allowed to eat or drink for a week at a time, and then discovered that they had been caught secretly drinking water, we would not be surprised because we know how impossible it is to live without food or drink. The same is true of our sexual nature. It cannot be ignored.

Unhealthy repression is bound to exhibit itself in an illicit manner. Likewise, importing within our marriage a religious sexual piety beyond the reasonable and legal limits of the actual ancient teachings is counterproductive to the bonding experience which must take place between husband and wife. The definition of holiness in sex is anything which serves to bring a husband and wife closer together, barring intentional destruction of seed (and sex during the menstruation and a week thereafter). But barriers which separate a husband and wife should always be avoided.

The religious wife in the story that began this chapter has, of course, every right to refrain from oral sex if it is something she personally feels uncomfortable with, and a husband should never push his wife to do anything that repels her. But that still doesn't mean that he can't try, lovingly, to persuade her about doing things which will bring them mutual pleasure. Yet neither spouse should base their objections to a sexual position on piety because religion desires husbands and wives to be totally satisfied with each other sexually. Far from being an exalted level of piety, prudishness in marriage is a sin which might push spouses to explore, either directly or through fantasy, other possibilities outside the marriage.

5. Married people and masturbation

Masturbation is the thief of love.   Tim and Beverly Lehaye

Don't knock it. It's sex with someone you love.   Woody Allen

A woman occasionally is quite a serviceable substitute for masturbation. It takes an abundance of imagination, to be sure.
                                                    Karl Kraus (1868-1962)

Once during an Oxford debate against a psychosexual counsellor, my opponent launched a diatribe against me for offering that masturbation lessened our dependency on our partners. She was adamant that, on the contrary, the more we masturbate, the better our sex lives become. 'Practice makes perfect,' as she said numerous times. 'People who don't masturbate are the most sexually repressed people around and they are also the worst lovers and have not begun to surmount corrosive sexual inhibitions.' Moreover, she said, frequent masturbation allows us to experience pleasure and discover what is most gratifying to us. 'Those who do not masturbate do not know themselves.'

It just goes to show how emotional the issue of masturbation is. For most of us, however, the issue is less high-principled, if not downright banal. David, a chairman of a multi-national corporation who I came to know through the L'Chaim Society, favoured masturbation because he travelled constantly and was sometimes out of the country for six weeks at a time. Although he was trying to become more religions, he scoffed at any prohibition against masturbation.

'Tell me what you think is better, Shmuley. I have to go on long business trips for long stretches. We have two small children at home, so my wife cannot always accompany me. Is it better that I sleep with strange women while I'm away, or that I masturbate to those blue movies they have in hotels nowadays. I would never cheat on my wife, but I'm not made of wood. I need some sort of sexual release.'

His argument gave me an opening. 'Who says that you are meant to be away from your wife for weeks at a time because of business? You are telling me that you're not made of wood and you need sexual release. You get it through autoeroticism which allows you to be away from your wife for a long time. But if you refrained and had no sexual outlet other than your wife, you would have to come home. Your marriage is more important than your business, and your sexual dependency on your wife, when she is your only outlet, reminds you of that always.'

Masturbation isn't worth it

Masturbation is certainly not kosher. But since virtually every world religion incorporates some prohibition of masturbation, most people who come across these prohibitions are convinced that they represent everything which is primitive and anti-quated. The same conclusion is drawn from the fact that society invented its own taboos against masturbation, such as the myth that if men, and especially girls masturbate, they will go blind or enormously increase the size of their genitalia (sorry guys, it doesn't work). As a result, in the modern world those who don't masturbate are considered about as enlightened as cavemen.

The most common modern argument in favour of masturbation, and one which is advanced almost exclusively by female experts, is that it is entirely unfair that a woman should (a) have to serve as her husband's exclusive outlet for sex, and that (b) a wife should not have to wait for her husband to pleasure her, which most of the time he fails to do anyway. Many women dislike, even detest the fact that their husbands use them constantly to gratify themselves and see it as a burden. They especially hate 'the quickies,' whereby a husband initiates the sexual act with no thought whatsoever as to whether his wife is even interested, but because he feels lusty.

Why should a wife have to suffer through these most casual encounters? Isn't if far better for a husband who craves sexual release to go off and masturbate, instead of forcing his wife to undress for something that barely involves her? Likewise, why should a wife have to wait for her husband to make her feel good? Since most surveys contend that women have far stronger orgasms masturbating than in sex with their husbands, why should this pleasure be denied them?

Technically faithful husbands

Often, the problem with experts is that they focus on details and miss the bigger picture. Like the perception of masturbation, unfortunately, love and relationships have changed in the modern era. Whereas once they were about two people who needed each other finding comfort in each other's arms, today they are about two people who enjoy each other, sharing as much time as will allow them from their mutually hectic lives.

Granted, David's recourse to masturbating is far better than sleeping with his female colleagues or secretaries. But even so by his actions he is still making a grave mistake. What he is doing is not neutral and harmless, but rather has grave consequences for his marriage. One of the most beautiful moments of marriage is when a husband and wife who are forcibly separated, for reasons of business and other reasons, long and look forward to being together in the same bed again throughout the period of separation, and then actually reunite. There are few moments as passionate or as powerful as that night when all the pent-up sexual pleasure erupts.

David, however, is allowing all of his sexual steam to escape through cracks and creaks. He is not building up any libidinous sexual reserve, all of which could later be focused exclusively on his wife for intense pleasure. And imagine how his wife feels. If he were not sitting in front of these blue movies which serve as a sexual vent, he would return voraciously hungry for her. He would grab her when they arrived home in private, and she would feel like the most desirable woman in the world.

But as it now stands, he arrives home, after releasing himself on several occasions, gives her a little peck on the cheek, asks what's for dinner, and jumps in bed to watch television, and their life remains unmarked by their long separation. In a sense then, he has cheated on his wife because he is meant to make her feel loved and attractive. He has failed to produce the goods.

Enjoying is not the same as *needing*, and I don't think that today's men and women depend on each other nearly as much as in the past. Indeed they fear doing so. This is why, when things go rough, relationships so frequently crumble and die. Two people who need each other don't run to the divorce courts whenever they have a problem. They find it difficult to conceive of life without the other. They cannot function without each other.

Marital fights

A true test of the health of any marriage is the effects which fighting has on the participants. If husbands and wives can go days on end without making up – if he can sleep on the living room couch with no inner compunction to come back to his wife's bed – their marriage is in serious trouble. But if they cannot work or concentrate until they make up – if they can't sleep through the night after a quarrel – even if this sometimes means that they continue to have more heated exchanges because they are obsessed with their current estrangement, the marriage is strong.

This need is a very deep love that may not express itself through the couple drooling over each in other in airport lounges. On the contrary, it is far more deeply rooted than that. But it does express itself in the form of a profound dependency, a helplessness and vulnerability that only one's spouse can satisfy. Like the hunger that leads a ravished man desperately toward food, so too the man or woman starved for each other's affections gravitate toward one another, overcoming every barrier. True emotional need expresses itself in a very physical way, in which you just have to hold onto and display intense affection to the object of your love.

It cannot be denied that when we make our spouse into our principal, and hopefully, only sexual outlet, we will treat them far better and act far more nicely. And just as you never shout at your bank manager because you need him, you never shout at your wife because you need her for pleasure and excitement. And if she withholds her sexual favours because she is upset, you have nowhere else to go. So you better kiss and make up. The alternative of finding an ongoing outlet in masturbation makes our libido into a punctured balloon, slowly loosing all its steam, that has no ability to rise.

When our sex drive is interrupted it no longer has the strength to propel us to our spouse. David in the story above told me of the deteriorating state of his marriage. He then began to analyse its causes. 'We're fighting a lot more now than ever before. Part of the reason, I guess, is all the pressures we have. We both work, and with two kids and a mortgage, we blow off a lot of steam in each other's direction.' But then he said in a moment of total honesty, 'I also find that I argue with my wife far more when I masturbate.' But when he really wants sex this need expresses itself in the very sensitive way that he treats her.

We must try and remember that masturbation is not a solitary practice, or a private matter with which public pronouncements on morality are unconcerned. It lessens the necessity for physical closeness which one human being feels for another. It is beyond the realm of the private and personal and is squarely an issue with which others are involved. Every act of masturbation serves as a powerful sexual release that in turn lessens our vital need for sex with someone else, and in the context of marriage this is disastrous.

6. Should sex be used to mend bridges?

More than a physical trip, lovemaking to me, is a mind healer. It erases all the tension and conflict built up between you and your partner during the normal course of living. It also strengthens your image of yourself, as an acceptable, loveable person.

A husband responding to a magazine survey

I notice that while sex doesn't solve any of life's other problems, it often acts to take the edge off them – sort of a tranquilliser.

A wife responding to a magazine survey

A little coitus never hoitus.   Anonymous

For a man and woman to live together under the same roof and have to share everything is a highly unnatural state, and some bickering and fighting is to be expected. Yet, however natural it may be to squabble, there are two obvious objectives which every couple must set before their sights always. The first is, obviously, to keep arguments to a minimum, and the second is to end the altercation as soon as possible. In helping two human beings to be forged together and live as one flesh we must do our earthly part. And few things in achieving the objective of ending squabbles as quickly as possible, are as powerful as lovemaking.

Couples should first of all use sex to mend arguments. Only sex brings in its wake a tidal wave of overwhelming positive emotion that makes a husband and wife feel intensely good about each other, washing away any hurt or friction that has been caused. In ending arguments, sex is the most powerful tool in our armoury. And it should be deployed as much as possible.

Yet, many people disagree, and this opinion has elicited a lot of angry response. The wives have pointed out that this is a typical male thing and that it doesn't resolve any of the problems. They feel used when their husbands refuse to talk a problem through and instead want to kiss and make up. And others have, for example, pointed out that one of the prohibitions in Jewish law is making love to one's spouse while the couple is fighting or angry at one another. It would seem therefore that both things make sex after or during a quarrel supremely unkosher.

Why then do I still affirm this advice?

Sexual healing

Coming from a broken home, I sought advice from everyone I possible could before I got married. What is the secret of success in marriage, I asked them? I was surprised at how much people were willing to reveal about their own relationships and marriages and what they had learned along the way. Some of my friends were even kind enough to take out pictures and diagrams of intimate moments with their wives to help me get the picture (OK, this isn't completely true, but it came pretty close).

I particularly remember speaking to the wife of a very close friend who gave me the following advice: 'When you get married you will no doubt argue,' she said – and I knew that her marriage had been particularly stormy – 'and there will be a tendency to kiss and make up and solve the problem through love-making. But don't do it. It doesn't solve anything. The cause for the argument is still there, in fact, stronger than ever, and all you are doing is covering it over for the time being with some tarmac. And even though at the time it feels great, it's just an escape. When it's over, the problem still exists and has to be resolved.'

However, ten years, thank all-merciful God, and six children later, I think the advice was wrong. It is the squabble that really paves over the latent love between man and woman. For why should problems be allowed to stand in the way of the deep feelings the couple have for each other? Isn't the truth of the matter that men and women are different, and will always be different, and that resolving any and all outstanding issues between them is clearly impossible?

Amidst the unbridgeable gap that separates them, what brings men and women together in the first instance is their attraction for each other, which pulls them closer despite their differences. And what keeps them together in the long term is the love that develops through sharing a life together after the initial attraction. Similarly, the one thing which brings the marriage back on track after a fight is the raw sexual attraction which brought the couple together in the first place, to remind them of their love for each other.

Satan is a hired gun

There are two ways of looking at arguments between husbands and wife, in much the same way that there are two ways of looking at sin; and here I take a step back from being an author about sexual intimacy and don my ecclesiastical robes to explain myself.

One can either view sin – doing something wrong – as being something real that must be eradicated and dealt with seriously, or as something unreal, merely concealing and covering goodness, like a thick fog that obscures the light. Here lies one of the major points of departure between mainstream Christianity and Judaism. In the Christian scheme of things, God is opposed by a rebellious and fallen angel who has set up for himself an alternative kingdom. In the same way that God promises rewards for good deeds, the devil promises material plenty for those devoting themselves to his will in place of the divine. The two powers compete against each other for human followers, and although ultimately God will prevail, the devil has free reign in the meantime.

Hence, if one has committed a sin, it is insufficient just to turn one's head from the lapse and continue on the path of righteousness. Since sin is real one must first obliterate the sin. The individual must liberate himself from the devil's grip through confession, deep remorse, and even chastising the body and self-flagellation have been suggested for this. God, according to Christianity, even sent his own son to bear the terrible consequences of human sin which could not be removed through human agency.

But this type of thinking is not part of Jewish thought, which is holistic and can accept no powerful ruler save the Almighty Himself. Goodness is defined as the proximity to God, and evil is defined as being distant from God. Actions which bring us closer to God are defined as good, while actions which remove the divine presence from us are evil.

Although Judaism also speaks of a 'Satan' which lurks in the heart of each individual, the Zohar explains that this Satan, or evil inclination, should more properly be seen as a hired agent of God. While attempting to lead humans away from the path of righteousness, he secretly hopes that the individual will not succumb to his seduction. Satan is a trusted agent of God whose purpose is to confound man with choices so that humans, exercising their freedom of choice, can improve their moral stamina by refusing to do the wrong thing.

Judaism, therefore, says that our focus in life should be not on the bad things we have committed, but on all the good things we failed to do while pursuing the bad things. While there is confession in Judaism, such as the penitential prayers on Yom Kippur, this serves merely to help us identify what we have been doing wrong, and truly regret our selfish actions, so that we can correct our course *for the future*. Jewish penitence serves only as a means by which the sinner is sensitised to his wrongdoing.

In order to destroy even the gravest sin one must look forward and simply do a 'mitzvah', a good deed. Every sin of commission is in reality a sin of *omission*. It's not that you've committed a wrong. Rather, you omitted to continue on the correct path. Remorse is too great an indulgence in sin and bestows upon the past far too great an importance. Sin is dealt with mainly by drowning it in a sea of light, in an ocean of goodness

How about marital transgressions?

What we must try and recognise in marriage is the power of even one good deed in our spouses to bring back our love for them. For many years I have observed how the clearest obstacle to Oxford students becoming seriously involved in the observance of Judaism is that they say to themselves, 'I've missed the boat.' 'It's too late for me to begin now.' 'I'm already set in my ways.' But, twenty five years of not living a Jewish life pales into insignificance when one performs even one mitzvah and allows the light of the human soul to illuminate one's life. And the same is true of marriage.

Even if a husband and wife have a huge amount of negative baggage, they can reverse so much of it with a single romantic gesture. Lapsed relationships that have died with neglect can be immediately resurrected with one loving act. Little romantic gestures like bringing home flowers or kissing a spouse when they least expect it, can remove so much accumulated pain, and can be far more powerful than words.

It is for this reason that I oppose the advice given to me by my friend and believe that couples should use the power of physical love to end most (though certainly not all) forms of marital bickering and strife. To deal with marital altercations in other ways is, in my opinion, to lend too much credibility to an argument about who did what wrong, and arguments don't deserve this credibility. Most marital altercations revolve around petty insensitivities which mushroom into full-scale conflict and stating that we should not just kiss and make up suggests that there is a real problem.

'You don't love me'

To be sure, if a husband and wife are in a heated argument over very serious allegations, such as infidelity or physical or even severe verbal abuse, this is a grave matter indeed which certainly cannot be solved through the sharing of a bed on its own, and I accept that in such circumstances my advice can be disregarded. It was for very weighty matters like these that the Talmud forbade husbands and wives to share intimacy when they are very angry with each other.

But most couples argue over the silliest things: why dinner wasn't ready on time, who should walk the dog, how much extra money a wife or husband has spent, why didn't you call me when you arrived at your convention, and this action of yours confirms my belief that you just don't take me seriously. Stated in other words, the overwhelming majority of arguments which ensue between married couples develop into full-blown battle precisely because it is treated by the other party as proof that their spouse does not really love or care for them.

A wife whose husband forgets to call her at an appointed time is not upset that he has not called. She can live without the phone call. Rather, in her mind this neglect is wider proof of the overall fact that he doesn't care about her. 'Perhaps it is true,' the wife says to herself, 'that my husband did not call me because he was too busy. But it's also just as likely that he didn't call because everything in his life is so much more important than me. Everything comes before me.' And she harbours this painful thought the whole day until he returns, and when he steps through the door, war breaks out.

A woman once told me that she and her husband had a terrible fight over the fact that he forgot to buy bread at the bakery on the way home from work. 'I reminded him three times, and he still forgot.' Did she really think that bread was worth fighting over? 'Of course not. But it just shows how he doesn't listen to a thing I say.' 'If he loved me, he wouldn't have forgotten.' But that is why I reiterate that the best way to undo her belief that he doesn't care – *that is, until the request arises again and he is afforded an opportunity to fulfil her request* – is to hold her and tell her how much he cares.

Fanning nascent love

Such problems, starting as petty trivialities, must be stopped before they develop into something far more serious. The fact that a husband omitted calling, forgot to buy bread etc., displayed not a sin, but an omission to show her love. He should be allowed to hold his wife and assure her that the cause of his neglect was stupidity. He simply didn't think. And the solution, then, is to show how much you are dependent on the other and have awaited your reunion throughout the day, and make love.

We who live in the post-sexual revolution world, are hit everyday by sex gurus with their endless advice of how the essence of a relationship is good communication. Indeed 'talking' and sharing ideas have become the idols of modern marriage. Most people today aspire to be music lovers, museum lovers or any other type of lover, rather than just plain lovers. One man even told me that he and his wife are supremely compatible because both love riding horses (I asked him whether sharing the common experience of sitting on the ass of a horse is really sufficiently profound to make people happy?) But, though good communication is essential to a marriage, it will never have the same effect of making someone feel intensely wanted through a physical embrace.

Even a husband and wife who are fighting horribly really do cherish each other. But their deep emotions, their fiery love, has grown dim from the pain of constant bickering. Like fire in a coal, their love has receded and by fanning the spark of their inner emotion and making love, their true feelings re-emerge and stability is restored. Communication is no substitute for these feelings of closeness which are brought to the fore when they make love out of mutual desire and respect. When a couple decide to kiss and make up, and once again become one flesh, they are making a very important statement that, essentially, there is nothing fundamentally wrong with their relationship.

7. Sex, when to refuse it

It's always me who has the gripe, me who wants to make the point. There's never any resolution of our bickering.

I always initiate talking about the problem. I think of what I'm going to say umpteen times, and then finally spit it out because I can't stand the silence anymore.
> Two women in the *Hite Report on Female Sexuality*, 1981

Men say women can't be trusted too far. Women say men can't be trusted too near.
> Anonymous

Do you know what virgins eat for breakfast. No, I didn't think you did.
> Anonymous

There are a number of important caveats to my advice about the use of sex in arguments which I would like to add in response to accusations, mostly from informed women, that sex is counterproductive in solving a dispute. To their very legitimate complaint that they cannot be tender to a man who has just been so harsh, I say that I of course concur. There are certainly many marital problems which really are far more serious than I have thus far allowed.

If a spouse, for instance, has a very bad temper, yelling and screaming all the time, it can certainly destroy the marriage. If a wife is spending far more money than the couple can afford and her husband agonises day and night about how they will pay their bills, this too can undermine their union. If a spouse is perennially late for important engagements, it can irritate their partner to no end. As stated above, the ancient Rabbis, in fact, prohibit a couple to share intimacy if either party is aggrieved or angry at the other. In these circumstances a husband must first apologise for any verbally abusive behaviour, utterly renouncing his actions and beseeching his wife for pardon.

And don't get me wrong, I don't mean that a husband can just wait to do better next time and that matters don't have to be discussed, or that a wife's anxiety over a given subject, and her need to discuss frankly and honestly and express her views, are not legitimate. The very meaning of a marriage is that you both seek to relate, to accommodate each other's requests and allay each other's fears. If a wife wishes to discuss an issue – whatever the issue – this is extremely important. But both spouses need to understand that timing is essential here.

Male reluctance to talk problems through

Earlier I mentioned that there is a real gender difference between the sexes as to how each copes with arguments. According to virtually every marital survey, it is overwhelmingly the men who want to employ lovemaking as a means by which to end a dispute. Sex researcher Shere Hite cites the astonishing statistic that 88 per cent of women say the men in their lives seem to prefer to avoid 'talking things over,' rendering a fight inevitable.

She quotes the frustration of many women. 'The usual pattern is, he makes me furious, I sound off, he says nothing, finally I demand that he say something, he says, "What do you want me to say?" which makes me more furious because I still don't know what he is thinking about whatever I'm so upset about.'

Many women will refuse to have sex with their husbands until they discuss the problem. They see having sex as a sign of their own weakness and capitulation. If the problem is a real one that will not go away, why should they be allowed to just kiss their way through it? And they get even more frustrated when they draw a blank. As a woman reported to Shere Hite 'He sits immobile, looking "above it all" ... while I try to get through to him. What really infuriates me is that he comes off looking like he is the one with "good manners," while I'm making a fool of myself, becoming emotionally out of control and hysterical.'

But sex is not an act of capitulation

Here I suggest that, although the husbands and the wives are both correct, the husband's way should be followed first, and not for reasons of male seniority or patriarchy. If the problem is real and needs to be discussed, speaking about it while each party harbours hate and animosity toward the other will, in all probability, just make things worse.

Words can often be like throwing petrol on a fire, not least of all because in most cases both parties claim to be right. Making love, while not solving the problem, at least removes much of the immediate hate and resentment that this latest dispute has aroused. And it is a good and mature way of doing it. After this, however, the wife's way must be pursued. It is now time to talk things through. Now that you are reminded of how much you really mean to each other, it is time to seriously address your differences and seek a logical and well-thought out resolution.

A husband who feels his love for his wife will endeavour to accommodate her, and not upset her. It's only if he feels angry or irritated that he will not do so. Neither of you will go out of your way to accommodate a stranger. But you will go out of your way to accommodate your spouse. So, in order to achieve the desired outcome, you should undertake the kind of activity that reminds you that you are partners, and you do not seek to argue with them, so much as do something which is mutually beneficial for your married life together.

These words stem from a fundamental Jewish mystical belief that in truth, deep down, we are all essentially good people and all we need is to remove the 'klipah', the husks or shells, which conceal our innate goodness. And included in this belief is that any couple who once professed love for each other can recapture that love if they only try just a bit harder, instead of getting bogged down in the quagmire of their problems. Sex has this awesome power and can really draw a couple closer together again. In Jewish thought, this is the ultimate purpose of sex.

Never move out of the bedroom

For this reason spouses should never sleep apart. Two married friends of mine, Denise and Steven, had a massive argument because Steven sits in front of the TV when he comes home, and Denise claims that he is totally inattentive to her, being completely absorbed by his TV programmes. Although this has been a constant source of irritation to Denise it really came to a head when a close friend of hers called with an important message while she was out. Steven, who was watching TV, answered the phone, and promised to pass on the message when his wife got home. But he forgot.

Denise was furious when she discovered the next day that her husband couldn't even be bothered to write the message down. When she saw that her husband refused to discuss the problem seriously, she decided that that night she would sleep in her daughter's room. Several times Steven tried to cajole her into returning to the matrimonial bed, but she refused. He tried to hug her, but she pulled away. Unfortunately, her stubbornness just provoked the same reaction in him, and for three days they didn't speak to one another.

I asked Denise, 'Do you believe your husband loves you?' 'Yes,' she said, 'but he's selfish. He is absorbed into himself and acts as if I don't exist.' I said 'Of course you shouldn't be a doormat, and he must show you respect. But there is a fine line between standing up for yourself, and taking revenge. Why should he desire to accommodate a woman who is acting like a stranger to him, even if he deserves it? Just as you weren't going to share a bed with him because he acted like a stranger, you chose to become a stranger to him. He's definitely in the wrong, but do you want to be happily married, or do you want to be right, come what may?'

Kissing and making up does achieve two very important objectives in marriage. The first, which I have already mentioned, is that it reminds a couple amidst their current difficulties just how much they truly love each other, even if five minutes before they felt that they hated each other. But, the second thing it does is to convince us firmly that we are entirely capable of taking control of our lives and that petty squabbles are nothing but momentary irregularities in an otherwise healthy, loving relationship.

When couples should not have sex together

Let me reiterate, I am not in any way implying that making love before resolving problems is applicable in all cases. On the contrary, there are undoubtedly matters of the most serious nature which must be resolved, and whether or not we follow this advice depends on the degree and the seriousness of the argument.

There is no reason in the world, for example, why a wife who has discovered that her husband has been unfaithful should allow herself to be touched by her husband until proper penitence is performed on the part of the husband and he has received his wife's full forgiveness, renouncing any and all contact with the other woman. Similarly, a wife who is physically hit by her husband would be crazy to submit to his affections, before serious discussion, and counselling has been undertaken for this most humiliating and deplorable of actions.

Why this won't apply in most cases

But let me reiterate here too that 90 per cent of all marital disputes are over very petty matters that do not come close to the items just mentioned, and we dare not give them greater credibility than they deserve. One of the proofs I use to demonstrate to couples that their marital rows are not half as serious as they think, and that with a little tenderness, affection, and of course, communication, things can be resolved, is this: instead of listening to the lengthy deliberations, I simply ask 'What were you arguing about?' Most of the time, they are embarrassed to say what led to the argument – to the point where they will usually embellish the cause – because objectively speaking it either wasn't terribly important, or was avoidable.

And so, if the husband and wife are genuinely sorry, there really is no problem. The best way to undo a belief that my husband or my wife doesn't care – that is, until the request arises again and one is afforded an opportunity to fulfil one's spouse's request – is to hold them and express how much you care and what you mean to each other. The one caveat is, as I said in the previous chapter, that in the interval immediately after the argument and just before lovemaking, the offending party (or parties) must offer a sincere, and full apology for their insensitive actions. But lengthy discussions before physical love will usually exacerbate rather than solve the problem. A prolonged discussion is essential, but only once you have healed the wound and you have both calmed down.

8. Does size matter?

I'm tired. Send one of them home.
> Mae West, on being told that ten men were
> waiting to meet her in her dressing room

Love is the delusion that one woman differs from another.
> H.L. Mencken

The students of Oxford who hear how Chassidic Jews abstain from sexual relationships before marriage, even once they are engaged, find the whole concept ludicrous. As one student said to me, 'How did you know that you were compatible? Didn't you feel that you had to check out the merchandise, you know, like test-drive each other?'

My favourite reply to them is that those who are fortunate enough to have had only one, or few, sexual partners, or to have married one of the first people they dated, have no other criteria by which to judge their partner other than their happiness. For them, whether or not they are emotionally and sexually satisfied in their marriage has only to do with their own, personal feelings, and not with an objective, universal standard.

Rather, the only thing they need to know for a good sex life is whether or not *they* feel satisfied and happy. The strongest synonym for love is 'subjectivity,' but the sexual openness and experience of today's world has allowed every husband and wife to evaluate each other objectively. Those who have retained some innocence and naiveté in the intimate areas of their lives are the ones who enjoy uncomplicated and pleasurable moments of natural love because their relationship is not haunted by memories of previous lovers.

One of the greatest problems of modern-day relationships is that men and women have dated and slept with so many people that most men have become experts on women, and women experts on men. This expertise inhibits the natural bonds of love that come automatically to those who have no criterion by which to compare. A man need not know at all whether his wife's curves are perfect, and a woman need not be able to objectively gauge whether her husband is great in the sack.

For couples who first sleep together only after marriage the experience of sex will always be pleasurable. They are not seeking to perform or attain a high rating. Their focus is not on 'How am I doing, I wonder what she thinks of me,' but rather on 'How can I make her enjoy this experience as much as possible, so that she feels how much I love her and want to be with her.' A couple who live in this mould gain everything, and have at least as thrilling a time as anyone else would have had, without sacrificing or compromising themselves.

The sexual Olympics

I know this is a far cry from the modern age where the first experience of young people is no longer of sex as a natural and loving act, but rather as a test of their own accomplishments and prowess. Men take women to bed with the purpose of not showing love, but winning competitions. 'Once women have me, there's no turning back.' They cannot seek refuge in the arms of their lover or spouse, for fear that if they engage in an act of love without being fully up to par, the judges will point their thumbs down. Even after the exertion of every effort on our part to please our partner, they still might feel dissatisfied because 'It was not as good as it was with Henry.' So, Jane and Alex spend the night together. In the morning Jane takes out her score card and gives Alex only a six for his efforts. 'A six,' he protests. 'How can that be? Why, I have been practising all week!'

But, what is left to us then? What sanctuary can we find where we just love and be loved remaining completely natural, just being ourselves? The whole beauty of sex, and what makes it mankind's most pleasurable undertaking, is that we put ourselves on autopilot, doing whatever comes naturally. Truly pleasurable sex is when it is entirely instinctive, rather than premeditated, where sex is a response to an urge, rather a forced and planned action. In job interviews we seek to impress, and at cocktail parties we seek to make others laugh, and on the sportsfield we seek to demonstrate our physical prowess. But in sex we simply celebrate the art of being and existing, rather than doing or performing.

Fear of rejection will bring in its wake inhibition will which cause us to either freeze up, or make sex into a show, an exhibition. Premarital sex leads, in my experience as Rabbi, to relationships in which sex is no longer an intimate moment, but rather a rat race to sleep with as many partners as possible. Everyone has been intimate with many bodies, and couples can no longer enjoy their love-making without allowing for the thought that they will be judged and compared with the men and women who preceded them. One can only shudder at the thought of so many people feeling inadequate because of drooping biceps, pot-bellies, or the size of their breasts or genitals.

Feeling underendowed

Having been told by one of her friends that a male acquaintance was six foot and seven inches, Mae West is said to have replied 'Let's forget about the six feet and talk about the seven inches.' Studies show how right she was. Rather than live by the dictum of 'What matters is not the length of the wand, but the magic in the stick,' it appears that no less than 80 per cent of men are dissatisfied with their size.

I was aghast to read in the *Hite Report on Male Sexuality* that, typically, 'men wished over and over again that their penis could be just a little larger.' Men appear to have the strangest hang ups. One of the interviewees (with an appendage rising to the national average) said: 'I think it is a good size when by myself, but in the presence of other men I feel self-conscious … It is as if I am underdeveloped … Emotionally, I feel I am a boy in a world of men.' Another offered '[Mine] is big enough, but I'd like it to be even bigger, so that a woman would gasp when she saw it.'

This preoccupation is a frightening reflection of the modern

mind set. In 1994 CNN carried a story of a respected surgeon in
the United States who now makes a fortune performing an
operation which elongates the penis. He extracts fat from the
body and guarantee that by surgically implanting the fat at the
end of the penis, it will be approximately 30 per cent longer. But
the odd thing about the operation was that, when interviewed,
the same doctor said that the majority of the men who have the
operation are already average size. Only in two circumstances did
he have anyone undergo the operation whose size was below the
national average.

Female angst

Women suffer no less in this modern beauty contest of the sexes.
Bonnie and Andrew had never had an easy relationship, even
before their marriage. Within six months Andrew came to see me.
He complained that Bonnie was irrational. She always turned the
lights off before sex, and would freeze up the moment he put them
back on. I asked him if he had done anything to make her feel so
self-conscious, and he denied that he had.

But in speaking to his wife it turned out that every time they
watched TV together, he would always comment on how beautiful
the actresses on the screen were. The same was when they went
out with married friends. Andrew would often comment on how
attractive other women were. 'But he never speaks to me that
way, so I feel ugly. He's always telling me that I have to lose
weight. I can't compare to the women he's attracted to, so I don't
want him to see my body.'

No wonder, then, that so many books which deal with sex and
human relationships advocate that the only way in which two
people can actually enjoy their intimate life together is by first
discarding all inhibitions relating to performance. To lead a
happy life, each of us needs a healthy dose of inner strength and
self-confidence. We have to have faith in ourselves as individuals
who have a unique gift to offer and this self-confidence comes
about primarily from the stability of a long-term relationship in
which our lover makes us feel like the most special person in the
world.

An affair as a quick fix

Today's arbitrary approach to marriage in which people treat their spouse as just someone they met, and with whom hopefully it will work – but if not, there's plenty of other people out there – leads to people discarding their marriages when difficulties arise. Once these spring up, they don't seek to sort them out, you just seek someone new. Just as a suit that shrinks after dry cleaning must be exchanged, or a toy that is scratched must be returned the thinking goes that a husband or wife who seems no longer as attractive, whose skin shrinks with old age, and develops bags and wrinkles, must similarly be replaced. If not permanently, then at least occasionally by having an affair. And this assumption insinuates itself quite automatically nowadays.

An accomplished female musician was telling me how she had never planned to have an affair. 'It just sort of happened.' She was happily married, but one of her fellow violinists with whom she toured 'just grew on me.' They consummated their mutual attraction one night in a New York hotel room, and their affair continued for a few months after that, until 'I got a hold of myself and knew that this wasn't for me since I love my husband.'

She went back to her husband, but their marriage has never been the same since. To be sure, their love for each other has remained strong, and they both say that they are happy. But it's their sex life that is as dead as a doornail. 'We share the same bedroom,' she told me. 'But we have haven't had sex together in more than two years, ever since a few months after my affair.' What went wrong?

She made it clear that the cessation of their sexual life together was at her instigation. 'I am sorry to say this, but my husband is just not as well-endowed as my lover was. And it's not true what they say, you know, that size doesn't matter.' 'Once you've had something really impressive, it's difficult to go back.'

'Now,' I asked her, 'If your husband felt the same way about you as your lover did, if he couldn't wait to get home from work everyday just to see you and lay eyes on you; if he stole away during the day and told you to meet him at hotels and the like and showered you with excitement and passion, would you have looked for a lover in the first place? 'I guess not,' she said, with a shrug of the shoulders.

What our age no longer understands is that our principal sexual organ is our mind, not our genitals. Sex is not about technique. It's about attentiveness and responsiveness. As Annette Lawson wrote, 'If the psyche is unwilling, no amount of technique can persuade it. And if the psyche is willing, no lack of technique can dissuade it.'

Disappointing sex

I even believe that those who indulge in many premarital sexual partners are actually worse lovers than virgins because they are accustomed to sexual gratification coming horizontally rather than vertically. Whenever they get bored of sex in an existing relationship, they simply exchange partners and move sideways, rather than digging deeper into the relationship to discover its untapped creativity.

And to what end? The benefit of a long education in sex is doubtful. In a debate on the legalisation of prostitution, Kathy, a twenty-something blond call girl who chaired a coalition of prostitutes, cried 'If you're a doctor you become an expert in medicine. I'm an expert in sex, and I'm damn good at it because of all my experience. I'm proud of what I do. On the contrary, how do you expect to be good at it if you don't do it? All these little Miss Mary virgins think they know what sex is, but they don't know nothing.'

I asked her 'Have you ever found any men that are as good at it as you.' 'No', she answered 'I must say all the guys I've been with are all boring drips. Classic disappointments.' And that was my point. Since she is such an expert, she has suppressed the capacity of being naive in sexual matters and being surprised and delighted at a man's sexual advances. Instead of determining whether some guy she loved just made her feel good, she instead focused on how well he performed, and she had the vast experience to make her an expert judge. She could never indulge in sex as a full participant, but rather as an objective observer.

But people still make the same mistake of capitulating to the ridiculous yet prevailing sexual norms of the age, and men and women will still feel inadequate as a result of their anatomy, not realising that by doing so they degrade their humanity. What men and women seek most in a relationship is the feeling that the person they are with is absolutely devoted and interested in them, and energetically passionate about them. *This* causes people to gasp, and draws them closer to one another. Not some superficial item of a person which might provide an initial shock which, since it is aesthetic and superficial, quickly wears off.

So what is the answer?

It is ludicrous to say that one can only be an exciting lover if one has many sexual partners. Good sex is all about initiative, creativity, spontaneity, being adventurous, loving, selfless, and never being lazy or rushed. All the things which one could try and learn from many sexual partners, one can experiment with within the context of a committed and faithful relationship. Read books, articles, speak with friends. Get ideas. Luckily, there many fascinating, detailed, and informative books on sex that can teach the aspiring lover and spouse anything they wish to know, and more.

But, most of all, ask your spouse what most pleases them. Never accept the totally fallacious argument that you can get from many partners what you cannot get from one partner. Isn't it enough that we all must constantly prove ourselves and compete in the marketplace, in the classroom, and in life in general outside the home? Life is full of competition whereby our standing as human beings, our potential for productivity, and our utility to those around us, is constantly called into question and rated. What we need, amidst this background of constantly proving ourselves, is a place where we can retire from the incessant pressure of everyday life, and into the arms of someone who loves us and wants to be with us just for what we are, rather than how we can be used.

The beauty of being married, of being in love, of having a family and especially parents, for that matter, is that our lovers and relatives just accept us for what we are. This feeling of what I call 'passive self-worth,' or feeling valuable even when we are not productive, is a human necessity. We need to be loved in an unquantifiable, immutable manner. We need to be told and to feel in our bones that no matter what we do and no matter where we go, there will always be those who love, cherish, and miss us. Without this, we are doomed to a life of anxious insecurity and agony. We should not be engaged in a constant state of *becoming*, but rather revel in the art of *being*.

9. What about pornography?

Obscenity is such a tiny kingdom that a single tour covers it
completely.   Heywood Broun

At male strip shows, it is still the women that we watch, the
audience of women and their eager faces. They are more obscene
than if they were dancing naked themselves.   Jean Baudrillard

Oxford is too small a city to have its own full-blown red light
district, but what it does have is a couple of pornography shops,
two of which, oddly enough, are both across the street from the
house where we lived for seven years. Considering the location, this
in itself is not surprising. Cowley Road is probably the most diverse
and interesting street in Oxford. There's the Inner Book Shop which
deals with alternative medicine, meditation, green publications and
the like, the Bangladeshi Mosque, scores of Tandoori, Jamaican,
and Halal restaurants, many second-hand clothing and book shops,
an anarchist tea house, bead shops, avant garde cafe's, the Jeho-
vah's Witnesses Temple – and of course the pornography shops (I
suppose it made perfect sense that the city's first Jewish Student
House should open in this district).

Both pornography shops are very low key, and stand just one
block away from each other as though huddling together for
comfort. One, the Private Shop, has no windows and is a strange
shade of blue. The other, the Adult Book Shop, was directly across
the street from our home, and advertises itself as selling 'marital
aids'. And, while the store front is entirely of glass, the glass is
dark and impenetrable to the interested gaze of the schoolchil-
dren who pass by, and is covered with wrought iron mesh. The
reason for this I discovered on one of our first mornings in Oxford.

While eating breakfast, we were startled to hear a terribly loud
crash: I ran outside to see the entire glass front of the Adult Book
Shop smashed to bits. I have since been told that this had
happened already many times, and that this is why one of them
has no window. The window-smashers are radical and not-so-
radical feminists and parents' organisations, who feel that the
shops are a cancer in the heart of Oxford. But, since the shops are
still there after quite a few years of concerted harassment, these

groups have tried other tactics, too. Probably the most successful one was to videotape every person who walked in. It served as a deterrent, but only until both shops set up rear entrances.

In search of passion

Now, to be honest, the shops are fairly unassuming. Moreover, a student who went there to buy me a not-very-amusing birthday present, which was found to be quite tasteless by most of the people who attended my surprise twenty-sixth birthday, told me that the shop is pathetically boring; nothing but shrink-wrapped plastic erotica and magazines, and certainly not very threatening. Nonetheless, the women in Oxford, particularly the students, often find the idea of a shop selling pornography, however pitiable its merchandise in reality, very offensive and generally demeaning.

Judaism, as one might expect, tends to oppose pornography. This is not because Judaism tows the prudish line of the religious 'right,' opposing pornography purely because it is indecent and immoral. Nor does it take the 'leftist' position that argues that it denigrates human sexuality and primarily degrades women. Although all these things may be true about pornography, they are not the root of the problem.

The issue for Judaism is that pornography does not enhance the passion and romance between a couple, but rather replaces them by something alien. As the purpose of sex is to foster and sustain emotional intimacy between husband and wife, whatever a couple does is permitted if it leaves their passion for each other intact. And here lies the problem, for in most cases pornography will serve as an end in itself rather than as a tool for the excitement of passion.

One of the most precious and important laws within the Jewish guidelines to love-making is that no spouse may think of another individual during sexual intercourse. If they do, then essentially they are violating the most precious gift given by God to us, the gift of human intimacy. For what kind of intimacy is it when you use someone's body as a mere form of friction for self-gratification, when you are thinking of and really being excited by the thought of someone other than your spouse?

A use for sex shops

One may, however, argue that the best way to rejuvenate a deadened sexual interest in marriage is to use pornographic aids. 'Agreed,' say those who argue this point, 'that pornography may not be the best thing for marriage, and really a couple should seek to be excited by each other. But what if that just doesn't happen. What if a wife really is bored by her husband's all-too-predictable sexual routine? And what if a husband just doesn't find his wife's flabby thighs alluring. Isn't it better that they should get excited through this, rather than sit and watch some boring television programme, and then turn off the lights and go to sleep?'

The answer is, yes. But there is a clear distinction between erotica and pornography. Any erotic device which causes us to be more focused on our spouse, however outlandish, may be used. An example of course is a wife buying the sexiest lingerie to excite and stimulate her husband. I even know of a very old and respected Rabbi from Russia, who, when a husband told him that he was losing sexual interest in his wife, gave him very explicit ideas about what he might buy (naturally, this Rabbi is very popular amongst his congregants).

And the same can be said of sexual devices and toys which allow a couple to expand their sexual play. This may not everyone's cup of tea, but that doesn't make it unkosher. Sexual toys and games may indeed be the answer for couples whose sex life needs to be raised from the dead.

If the Oxford shop described above could truly become what it purports to be, a marital aid shop, then the existence of such places should be applauded. Any device which helps keep a husband interested in his wife, and a wife interested in her husband, are praiseworthy. It does not necessarily mean that every couple should patronise and support them. Some couples may genuinely not feel the need to employ any external agents to enhance their sex life. But many do need it and therefore, every form of lingerie, mirror on the ceiling, or plastic object, which help us to break the pattern of monotony that can set into a relationship, are kosher.

We must all be realistic about the difficulty of maintaining passion in a monogamous relationship in which one has the same sexual partner day-in and day-out. And while intrinsic and internal causes for passion within marriage can of course be said to be far superior to external and artificial aids, this does not in any way limit their assistance in many circumstances and relationships and the fact that many couples would find them useful. Anything that can be done to help focus sexual energy on one's partner, or make love-making exciting and new, must indeed be done.

Pornographic magazines and videos

Nonetheless, I repeat, real pornography is very different. The same people may argue, 'What harm, after all, can there be in just watching other's people's bodies? After all, we're not really doing anything with them.' But any form of explicit sexual material which leads to a husband or wife focusing on someone or something other than each other is harmful. It is sexual excitement as an end in itself, rather than as a means to achieving enhanced closeness and excitement between two committed sexual partners.

The perfect relationship is where a couple have both passion, novelty, and excitement, on the one hand, coupled with intimacy, friendship, and predictability on the other. And while pornography may grant the former, it totally destroys the latter. It inhibits intimacy causing a man to be more excited by some stranger than his own wife.

When a husband watches some other woman on a celluloid screen and then makes love to his wife, he gives his wife his body but gives the image on the TV his heart and his mind. This is more like sexual decapitation, where he uses his spouse merely for glorified autoeroticism. Even if the thought of another woman might get a husband more excited during love-making with his wife, Judaism would not, could not allow this, and no self-respecting man or woman should tolerate it.

No wonder that in many surveys a vast majority of wives reject as cruel and insulting their husband's use of nude videos and magazines, even when it gets the husband interested in sex. Any means by which a husband blocks out his wife from his mind completely is degrading to her. If a couple watch a pornographic video while making love they are focusing on that video as the source of their excitement, instead of on each other. It is those external images which serve as the source of their passion. They may be making love while watching the film, but in spirit and in mind they might as well be with the people in the video.

Adultery of the mind

In this respect, pornographic magazines and videos are remarkably similar to adultery. In the case of actual adultery the chasm that is created is far more serious, since you have not only thought about sex with another partner or merely studied their body; you actually did something about it and shared an intimate act which is reserved exclusively for marriage. Nevertheless, because you fantasise about sharing intimacy with a stranger, it has the same effect of depleting some very necessary love from your marriage. You are focusing your pent-up sexual energy on some pornographic picture of a perfectly formed nude woman or man.

If there is no lust within their marriage, because it has been channelled elsewhere for too long a time, then the consequences will be that there is simply no marriage left to destroy. It has simply ceased to exist. If one's husband becomes to one as a stranger, then why continue to live with him when all he brings is grief? What really destroys a relationship is not the mistakes which a man or woman make to hurt their spouse. Rather, it is the emotional and erotic neglect.

The boom in home-made pornographic pictures

The truth is that we don't even really need pornography to get sexually stimulated when we feel bored with our spouse, and here is the proof. In the past few years, there has been an explosion of home-made pornographic material. The biggest sellers are not the professionally made, model and bombshell-ridden, videos of beautiful and shapely men and women yelling at the top of their lungs. Rather, it is ordinary housewives whose husbands film them doing none-too-professional stripteases and other voyeuristic acts.

In other words, what the guy down the street most wants to see is *your* wife taking off her clothes on film. So then, why are *you* bored of her? Of course the answer is, not that she is unattractive, but rather you have seen her a thousand times already and now you want to see something new. And seeing your neighbour Harry's wife Matilda take off her bra is damned exciting!

But you, and not your neighbour, should have those dirty thoughts about your wife. And act upon them. Rather than go out and buy one of these videos and magazines which are an insult to your wife, just go out together and get erotic things and acquire new ideas which you can do together and which bring the quality of newness into the marriage. Far better to take photographs or make videos of yourselves together, if you feel you truly need external aids to jump-start your passion, rather than that you both sit and watch strangers.

A brief word on modesty

It is sometimes argued that modesty prohibits certain sexual practices. But pious people, for example, who are dressing modestly because they think that lusting after the body is unGodly have got it all wrong. The Bible wants husbands and wives who lust after each other. The real reason that God commands us to dress modestly is so that the natural power of the human body to attract remains intact.

Sex must always be a journey of discovery that is fuelled by curiosity. Any other practice could lead to a scenario, whereby a wife comes into the bedroom and undresses while her husband is watching television. And even as she removes every stitch of clothing, he continues to watch television! When watching a BBC documentary on the western Amazon rain forest becomes more interesting than watching your wife undress, you know that your marriage has had it! Notice that the Ten Commandments prohibit a man from lusting after his neighbour's wife. It offers no prohibition against lusting after your own wife.

That this is the purpose of modesty, that is, to enhance rather than subdue the attraction of the human body and to increase the eroticism of the sexual encounter between husband and wife, is expressly related by Rabbi Menachem Meiri, one of Medieval Jewry's greatest Rabbis. He declares: 'Although a wife must be modest in public, her loss of all modesty in private is not a contradiction to this in any way, because the whole idea of her modesty in public is that she preserve her feminine charm for her husband.'

The point of sex

I once made the argument about pornography and sex aids in a closed seminar for Jewish married couples in London. Little did I know that there was a reporter in the audience. The next day, an Anglo-Jewish newspaper appeared with the headline: Rabbi Advocates Opening of More Sex Shops Around Britain. You can imagine that the next day I wasn't the most popular man in my religious Jewish community. So I wrote a letter to the newspaper correcting their report, and emphasising that I had supported the idea of marital-aid shops rather than sex shops.

A week later I received a letter from the owner of a string of sex shops asking if I would give my official Rabbinical seal of approval to these shops if they changed advertising and emphasised that their purpose was to aid married couples to get more excited about each other. He told me, 'I think that it would be great for business.' Well, I was prepared to go ahead with the outlandish idea, with three caveats. First, he had to rid the shops of all pornographic videos and publications. Second, he had to restrict access to married people. Third, he had to make me a 50 per cent partner in the business. He turned me down on all conditions.

The point is that the nature of human sexuality is something which pulls us outside of ourselves, instilling within us an outward gravitation, as it is meant to do. It is not at all something private or solitary. It is not something we can ever fully enjoy on our own. We must always contemplate someone else. Sexuality serves as the primary means of bringing two lovers together, and by inverting the process and using it for something other than this, if it is used purely for self-pleasure and not to attach us to someone else, we destroy the mechanism of binding two people as one.

10. Lights, on or off

And the eyes of them both were opened, and they knew that they were naked; and they sewed fig leaves together, and made themselves aprons ... and Adam and his wife hid themselves from the presence of the Lord God.   Genesis 3: verse 7-8

My advice to those who think they have to take off their clothes to be a star is once your boned, what's left to create the illusion? Let 'em wonder. I never believed in givin' them too much of me.'
                                                                    Mae West

A couple came to see me once. The husband was complaining about their sex life. 'My wife is too shy, it drives me crazy! I can't take it anymore. She insists on undressing in our bedroom with the lights off. And we can only have sex with the lights off. I can't be married to a prude.' His wife refused to discuss the matter with her husband present. But when he left the room she piped up, 'Of course I'll only undress in the dark. But it's his fault. He doesn't think I'm beautiful, doesn't even look at me. I undress and his eyes are still glued to the TV. I'm ashamed of the way I look so I only undress with the lights off. If he would give me more confidence I would be so much happier.'

The obsession we all have today to look like Adonis is often counter-productive to say the least. The husband spends three months living in a gym, but still his love-handles cling on to his body. The wife does everything to tighten her stomach, even using her children as weights to do sit-ups. But still her stomach and thighs seem to have a mind of their own. So they both become more inhibited during sex. The husband holds his breath the entire time, thinking that this way his pot belly looks muscular. But it doesn't work, and who needs this?

Staring and looking

The ancient Rabbis strongly advocated that love-making take place in the dark. There are other perhaps more profound reasons why darkness increases the mystery of sex. I don't often perform weddings, since I am more of an activist Rabbi who runs an

outreach organisation, but I had nonetheless agreed to marry
Jeffrey and Sally. Though they were not very observant, tradition
was important to them and we all agreed to study the Jewish
marriage laws together prior to the wedding. This actually put a
spanner in the works. Jeffrey saw that the Code of Jewish Law
says that a man should not stare at his wife's genitals, even
during lovemaking, and that love should be made with the lights
off. 'What kind of medieval nonsense is this? Once married, are
we meant to behave like two inhibited strangers? I can't even look
at my wife's body? This stuff's outdated rubbish,' he stormed.

'Notice,' I countered, as I said above, 'it doesn't say that you
can't look at your wife's body. Rather, it says that you shouldn't
stare.' In other words, don't get too hung up on each other's body
parts. Don't focus on genitals to the detriment of the total personality. Inhibition is brought into lovemaking specifically when the
body conceals the personality, and the biblical advice here is
never to allow that to happen in marriage. Sex should be about
the fusion of two personalities, rather than two bodies, and
physical attraction is merely a means to emotional love.

Bodily attraction is the bait

If we think about it, physical attraction is meant to work something like this: A man goes to a party. There is a woman nursing
a drink in a corner of the room. She catches his eye and he crosses
the dance floor to chat with her. What leads him across the room
is not her personality. He hasn't even met her! Rather, it's her
body and the chemical attraction that exists between the sexes.
Her comeliness serves as a magnet, pulling him toward her. The
more beautiful she is, the more irresistible she becomes.

But the purpose of her external attraction is to lead him to
come to know her inner beauty, her warm and engaging personality. For, notwithstanding how beautiful the body is, we grow
bored of discovering and rediscovering the body, because there is
not that much to uncover. If he sees her and just wants to have
sex with her, no relationship will develop. He goes over to her,
delivers his lines, and asks 'Your place or mine'. But if he wants
to know her, they can later become one. He first sees her body, he
walks over, and now he discovers her warm and engaging person-

ality, her easy and loving nature. What began as bodily attraction has been transmuted into the orchestration of two souls.

Personality is different to the body because it has depth. People are infinitely interesting. On a daily basis we all encounter new experiences yielding new insights. These can be shared with the person we love so that the relationship always has something to feed on. Layers of the soul open up to our beloved and reveal our essence. It is subject to horizontal and vertical change, encountering new experiences and gaining a deeper understanding of life. Sure, we may put on or take off a few pounds here and there, but this is hardly the stuff that matters.

Transcending the body

It follows, then, that in lovemaking our ultimate objective is to transcend the body. We experience an intense pleasure that makes us feel really good about our partner, the object of our love. We have an out-of-body experience. We feel transported by the sexual encounter, lifted above the constraints of the body and meeting at the level of the soul. This is what orgasm is all about. It is an intensely unifying moment in which man and woman experience a spiritual epiphany. But this is only true when the interest of pleasure are sublimated to become a tool of unity.

In the dark, where the sounds, movements, and feel of our beloved ignites the imagination and kindles the sensations, we are seeing with the eye of the mind. Fantasy is more easily integrated into the experience. This is why we so often close our eyes during love-making. And if closing our eyes allows us to pepper our sex lives with fantasy and imagination, how much more so does a darkened environment allow us to love fully and creatively?

Light during sex makes it so much more difficult to connect on that deeper level of personality, because the focus is still on the body. The casual sex we indulge in today is, therefore, not love-making but simple carnal relief. It is about whetting the appetite of the hormones and satiating the flesh. And this is why when it is over, we do indeed feel satiated. But we remain strangers and the next morning we feel an emptiness again. But love-making where the objective is the fusion of two personalities, leaves us hungering for more. We don't feel satisfied when it is over because we cannot get enough of our beloved, and we sleep sweetly in their arms. We have tasted, however momentarily, how beautiful it is to feel truly united with someone we adore, and we want more, and more and more and more.

The beauty of sex, as opposed to every other human activity, is that it is entirely instinctual. In sex, certainly unlike any public activity, people just let go. That which comes naturally overtakes us, and we feel ourselves running on autopilot. We are uncomfortable when we feel judged or the need to perform. We all hate taking examinations and job interviews. We know we are being evaluated, and it puts us on our guard. But when we can just totally let go in sex, surrendering ourselves to a person we love and trust, we come to know true ecstasy and pleasure. We glorify in the art of being and existing, rather than in becoming and doing. We are just being, not acting or behaving. It is the greatest joy of life, but it can only be achieved when we are least on our guard and at our most vulnerable.

Is there an ideal time of day to make love?

The ancient Rabbis were adamant that sex should take place well into the evening, at a time when husband and wife are relaxed and released from the cares of the world. And of course nowadays sex at night is also the most convenient: the children are asleep, Sainsbury's is shut, and the office is closed. Our minds are finally at rest. During the day we are focused on the millions of things we still have to do, our responsibilities tug at us and we have a complete agenda which still needs to be carried out. But at night we have little excuse but to focus intensely on our beloved.

If sex were only an act of the body, then it would be more appropriate for sex to take place during the day, when our bodies are least tired and our strength the most replenished. But our principal sexual organ is not the body. It is our mind. Only the mind can make something new. At nightfall it feels that we have accomplished whatever could be done, and that we have now earned the right to relax and experience loving pleasure.

This need not mean that a husband and wife should abstain from sex during the day, or at mornings when indeed their strength is at its peak. Indeed, the spontaneity of sex should never be compromised. However, we should be reserving our principal sexual moments for the evenings. Careless sex is just as casual inside of marriage as it is outside of marriage. Husbands and wives are not meant to have casual sex, where they make love to each other but are not utterly consumed by the experience.

The Talmud too advises, for example, that sex take place at night, but it also offers that one might have intercourse during the day, since otherwise the husband, overcome by sleep, might perform perfunctorily and end up despising his wife. Making love to a personality rather than a body must be coupled with the need for maintaining passion in lovemaking. The purpose of religion is for man to learn to fuse together and synthesise the Godly and the physical – his soul and his body – so that he become a Godly man. Similarly, the purpose of marriage is to fuse together the body of the husband and the body of the wife, allowing them to become one flesh. Only strong desire, which leads to pleasure and to union and love can achieve this.

Television in the bedroom

It should be pointed out that nowadays we are faced with a real problem. Television constitutes the strongest outside intrusion into a couples' sex life that I can identify. Offering entertainment which is always compelling (British and American television notwithstanding), it provides a strong alternative to an animated bedroom life. Giving a couple programmes that they must see and concerns that they have to discuss, it does little to pull a couple together through intimacy.

Later we will explore how, in Jewish thought, a husband and wife are not allowed to wear any clothing during sex. Sex is about flesh pressed against flesh with no physical barriers. But the same is true of psychological barriers. Psychological barriers are the strongest impediments to a total soul unity, and it is imperative that we rid our minds of all cares and concerns prior to sex. If we get into bed with half a mind, our spouses feel the distraction and are gravely insulted. Women especially want to feel that when they undress for sex, their husbands cannot help but get excited, drop everything they're thinking about, and make love to their wives.

Who can really sweet talk each other when the television is blaring, and who really needs the entertainment of sex when they have such other addictive entertainment? Any couple who are serious about sustaining passion in their marriages should greatly minimise the amount of TV they watch at night. Better yet, there shouldn't be a TV in the bedroom, but only in the kitchen or sitting room. One should avoid any unnecessary distractions in the bedroom, and so one should be cautious with those offered by modern technology.

11. Is prostitution a safe option?

Prostitutes believe in marriage. It provides them with most of their trade.   'Suzie' quoted in *Knave Magazine*

Prostitution gives her an opportunity to meet people. It provides fresh air and wholesome exercise, and it keeps her out of trouble.
Joseph Heller, *Catch-22*

Marriage is not a word. It is a sentence.   Anonymous

Whenever I debate the question of prostitution, and these debates come up surprisingly frequently, I always say that the people who should be asked their opinion on this question are those who are most affected by it, namely wives. It's bad enough that so many husbands show gross ingratitude to their wives by cheating. Most women who are on the game have the time to develop their physical appearance and sexual performance to a degree that the average wife, encumbered with numerous family responsibilities, does not. As one prostitute told me during a debate: 'I may not be a rocket scientist, but I can launch any man straight into orbit.'

Don't ask your wife to go along with it

Harry always complained about his marriage. Whatever spark had once existed between him and his wife had long since vanished. He murmured of lack of interest in sex. But he was a prominent member of his community who feared being shamed by divorce. Besides, he and his wife were close, if only as brother and sister. For the same reason he couldn't countenance an affair. What if he got caught? So he went to prostitutes instead. But he did so without any guilt because his wife Margaret actually condoned it.

I thought she had lost her mind. Her argument was that they had three children together, and got along quite nicely, even though their sex life had functionally terminated. The one thing she didn't want was to lose him, which she might do if he ran off with some other woman. With prostitutes there was little chance of that. Neither was there a real problem of disease, since Harry could easily afford to go to the really high-class ones who come with all the pedigrees. 'My husband's not made of wood,' she said and held this to be the best solution to a bad situation. She was afraid of divorcing Harry, so she allowed him to indulge his weaknesses.

Margaret may think that she is making the best of a bad situation, but really she is creating a bad situation. Rather than there being any hope of her and her husband one day rekindling their lost interest in each other, she is ensuring that their marriage has no future at all because she allows herself to be replaced with cheap substitutes. Her husband may need her cooking and conversation, but he doesn't need her as a woman. His masculinity is delivered over unto strangers.

Marriage, much more than a word

Since every marriage, even the dispassionate ones, have a nascent sexual fire, the objective of husband and wife is to fan it into a flame. A wife must not agree that the husband be allowed sexual outlets other than his wife, for in this way they will douse the flame together. He will no longer yearn for her in the same way he would if she represented his sole sexual outlet. If he cannot live with that, better that she throw the bum out than lose her dignity.

Marriage is a state of existence. Once that state has irretrievably broken down it is better to end it in deed than continue it in humiliation. It is far better to go your own way than destroy your self-confidence by inviting in competitors. The argument that men will go to prostitutes anyway carries no weight. What if Harry couldn't help beating the children. Would Margaret overlook that as well? People cheat on their taxes. Does that mean that we should legalise it?

Legalising prostitution

Every so often a provocative social commentator will agitate for the legalisation of prostitution and brothels. These often well argued pieces demand a coherent response. We cannot merely condemn something as being immoral or unethical and expect people to abide without demonstrating how what they think is beneficial is actually harmful without them realising it.

The oft-repeated arguments in favour of opening a legal brothel right in the heart of your neighbourhood are basically these: Men are going to go to prostitutes regardless of any other consideration. Almost 70 per cent of the men questioned for the 1948 Kinsey Report On Sexual Behaviour in the human male claimed to have visited a prostitute at some time in their lives. If brothels are legalised the risk of AIDS infection and the spread of sexual disease will be severely curbed, and the prostitutes themselves would be better protected rather than beaten by clients and pimps. Finally, if men feel that they need a sexual outlet with someone other than their wives, isn't it better that they go to a prostitute, where it won't lead to a full-blown affair, which might pull them away from their wives?

But all of the above are short-sighted arguments. The success of a society is based ultimately on the bonds between man and woman. If people who once professed love to each other and joined together in matrimony cannot live together in harmony, what hope is there for more far-reaching and abstract goals like world peace? Why on earth, then, would we want to make it easier for married men to cheat on, and thereby become less dependent on, their wives by guaranteeing them risk-free sex?

Sex represents the most powerful dependency of men on women. Instead of a man thinking that if he wants sex, he had better treat his wife with the greatest possible love and respect, here he can ignore her because a couple of quid will buy him his fantasies. What is the point of marriage if he can just go down the road to a brothel where the sex is exciting, the women screened for sexual disease, and where confidentiality is assured?

Overexposure

The greatest casualty of the permissive sex advocated and
adopted ever the since the sexual revolution of the sixties is
sexual eroticism itself. For sex to be exciting, there must be a
healthy dose of fantasy. Sex thrives specifically when it is somewhat concealed and hidden, when it involves the imagination. It
is like the negative of a photograph. It loses colour through
overexposure. This is why a body clothed in lingerie will always
be more erotic than a body which is completely nude. It invites
fantasy and exploration. And a healthy society will reduce the
amount of explicit material so as to retain the mystique of becoming one flesh.

It comes as no surprise that so many tourists who parade
through Amsterdam's notorious legalised prostitution district
describe the experience as evincing little more than a yawn after
the initial surprise. When men drive down a street and see
women who are almost naked selling themselves, it dulls rather
than heightens their interest in sex. It makes sex a commodity,
rather than something that must be striven before. After a while,
the men just drive by streetwalkers as if they were nothing more
than newspaper salesmen. The result is a society filled with guys
who have sex, but yawn while doing so.

12. Sadomasochism

> The aim of sadism is to transform a man into a thing, something
> animate into something inanimate, since by complete and absolute
> control the living loses one essential quality of life – freedom.
> > Erich Fromm

> Everyone probably thinks that I am a raving nymphomaniac, that
> I have an *insatiable* sexual appetite, when the truth is I'd rather
> read a book. > > Madonna

Upon the publication of my book, *The Jewish Guide to Adultery*,
friends of mine quipped that in time I would be forced to write a
sequel entitled, *The Jewish Guide to Incest*, or better yet, *The
Jewish Guide to S&M*. I thought this was rather a good suggestion at first, as I have always confused the initials S&M with

M&S, the initials of Marks and Spencer's, Britain's leading retail clothing chain. Since we Jews get an almost orgasmic thrill from shopping, such Freudian slips are not uncommon amongst us offshore islanders of the Mosaic persuasion.

Little did I know that two years later a television company would ask me to debate sadomasochism live with actual members of the Spanner case. The fifteen men who were prosecuted in this case for meeting regularly in Birmingham to mutilate each other's genitals in the name of sexual delight, had appealed to the European High Court of Human rights to overturn their convictions at the hands of the British court system which sent a number of them to prison. Lucky for us, they even videotaped their exploits for posterity, although never with the intention of public viewing.

But even their exploits are 'blasé and boring' by the standards of creativity adopted by some of the men I have spoken to through the proposed television programme. A young man named Mike enjoys lighting firecrackers in his bottom, and John likes hanging weights, and an occasional saw and other pieces of hardware, from his male appendage. Mike defends his sexual tastes with the following enlightened opinion: 'Most people have narrow views of sexuality. They see guys nailing their genitals to wood as disgusting. What's it got to do with them?' And Dominique Matrix from Feminists Against Censorship says about these activities: 'I love it. It's safe!' (as a dacha in Chernobyl).

What about consent?

The liberty for man to pursue any perversion he pleases is licensed by the argument from consent, or to be more precise, *informed* consent. What two consenting adults do in the privacy of their own bedroom is therefore beyond the letter of the law. As another television participant put it: 'It's up to individual adults what they do. What could possibly be wrong with it. It's a personal choice and nobody's else's business.' Others cry out against 'the sex police' and 'the purity patrol' and argue that it is highly immoral for society to intrude upon their private tastes.

But for consent alone to be used to defend these actions is manifestly absurd. Judaism cannot countenance the mutilation of the body under any circumstance bar one: when such actions

are undertaken expressly for medical purposes or the prolonging of
life, such as in the case of surgery under the knife. And Judaism is
no stick in the mud. Even cosmetic surgery is allowed on the pretext
that it brings for many substantial mental health and psychological
benefits. Mutilation of the body in the name of pleasure, however,
can never be right. Judaism believes the body to be a holy Temple,
even holier than the soul according to its mystics.

Sexual deviancy and genuine perversion

Yes, amidst the openness on sexual matters that I have argued
for throughout this book, I believe that sadomasochism is different, and constitutes a real perversion. Now, I hear you already
accusing me of intolerance. But hear me out.

As you I have made clear in the previous pages, I do not believe
that the human body is constructed for intercourse. On the
contrary, the human body is constructed for *reproduction*. What
percentage of sex actually involves copulation? Is kissing natural? Is that really what the mouth was made for? To slither down
someone else's oesophagus? Let's face it. Couples get up to some
pretty weird stuff anyway.

I think the concept of sexual deviancy is a contradiction in
terms. The essence of human sexuality is to do that which comes
naturally and automatically, we all have an intuitive gravitation
and orientation which we follow and which we find pleasurable.
And if sex is instinctual, then even strange sex cannot be considered a deviance because every person's instinct is different and
there is no norm. (I will ignore the religious question of homo-
sexuality for the laws are beyond any doubt on this point).

But sadomasochism is a real perversion because it is not
intuitive and is not propelled by instinct. Rather, it is all about
sexual experimentation, and is much like a heterosexual man
who has sex with another man, not because he wants to, but
simply because he wants to try something new and know what it
is like. The average person is not driven genetically to hammer
his scrotum to wood. It is an act which simply cannot be compared
to how a man or a woman are driven to adultery.

Sadomasochism results directly from our contemporary jaded,
fatigued, and overused approach to sex. Only when people have
become totally bored to death of sex in its natural and instinctive

form would they resort to such acts of desperation such as hanging pieces of hardware from their penis to jump-start sexual interest. Sadomasochism results entirely from the been-there-done-that mentality in which those who have no holiness or modesty in their sexual relationships will try anything to end the monotony.

Sadomasochism may be thrilling while it lasts, but it leaves the individual feeling empty and vacuous when it is over. Its participants are forced to expand, not vertically, but horizontally. They cannot get to know each other more deeply, rather they must resort to stranger and weirder sexual play in order to retain their interest. Instead of discovering deeper dimensions of each other's personalities and warmth, they try newer and newer adventures. And once that's done, they feel they must still expand their horizons further, until they go totally off the deep end – like sticking gerbils in places that are worse than any cage.

Desensitisation to violence.

When people partake of activities that are severely injurious to the human body, and call it a pleasure, they forfeit an ability to distinguish between that which is wholesome and good, and that which is agonising and hurtful. Violence, even of the self-inflicted variety, should never be dignified no matter what label it carries. The historical record of Rome is filled with lurid details of orgiastic excess and public displays of bestiality that accompanied its Empire before its fall.

As a Rabbi who hails from a religious tradition that has always glorified the sexual act between married adults, I am not a sexual prude. It is in the spirit of a profound respect for the loving bonds that sex can foster between two adults that these lines are written. But what two people do in the privacy of their bedroom is, of course, society's business if it leads to violence or turpitude, either directly, or indirectly. Even what a child watches on TV in the privacy of his own bedroom has a direct impact on society. This was the excellent point that Frances Lawrence made in her much-applauded manifesto after her headmaster husband was stabbed to death by one of the pupils in his school. Society as a whole must cultivate sex as an intimate and loving experience, rather than as a means by which two people use each other for experimentation, or even just plain pleasure.

13. Orthodox sex, a hole in a sheet?

He no play-a da game. He no make-a da rules.
Earl Butz, on the Pope's strictures against contraception

Question: What do you call people who use the rhythm method?
Answer: Parents.   Anonymous

When Jean-Marc and Lisa were opening their presents at their engagement party, everyone burst into laughter as they uncovered the present bought by his brother: a large white sheet, with a very small hole in the middle and a fluorescent light in the shape of an arrow pointing to the hole with the words: 'Insert here.' Jean-Marc was a law student at Oxford who came from a secular Jewish home, but he had become observant at Oxford. This had caused much consternation in his immediate family where they feared that he would change and become a fundamentalist fanatic. His engagement to Lisa, a highly likeable and not-too-observant American Jewish girl, had abated their fears somewhat.

Jean-Marc did not see the humorous side to this joke. The tension in the family was already high because of his return to orthodox religion, and he yelled at his brother that he had ruined his engagement party. 'Hey,' said his brother. 'I'm not the one who chose a religion that uses such sheets.' Losing all trace of humour, Jean-Marc exploded and yelled that this sheet nonsense had no validity to it and was just another way to discredit religious Jews, and he looked to me for backup.

'Actually,' I said, 'allowing a couple to have sex with a sheet with a hole in the middle is a very lenient Talmudic position. Some Rabbis actually insist on the husband and wife donning full body armour before sex, while others take it a step further and mandate that the husband and wife be in separate rooms while having sex through a hole in the wall. Still other Rabbis further to the right insist that they be in two different cities and have sex by fax.'

Flesh pressing against flesh

The real truth of the matter is that not only does Jewish law not mandate that a sheet be used, it even wouldn't allow it if the couple desired it out of a misguided sense of piety. The ancient Rabbis do not allow any articles of clothing to be worn during love-making. Sex must bring in its wake this tidal wave of powerful emotion that leaves a couple feeling closer, and this happens specifically through the powerful emotions awakened when the body is caused to tingle by contact with another body.

A couple can don anything they want during foreplay to arouse each other, be it lingerie, a French maid's outfit, or American football pads and helmet, if that's what tickles their fancy. But when full intercourse is achieved, it must be done without a stitch clothing so that there is no barrier to the intimacy which the couple achieve.

Contraception and condoms

This thought is further carried out in Judaism's opposition to condoms during sex. Judaism rejects Catholicism's extreme position that contraception is always morally wrong. There are many instances in which a couple are permitted to use contraception. Judaism, of course, insists that children are always a blessing, and therefore discourages a couple from using devices that impede pregnancy (at least until they have a boy and a girl who can themselves one day propagate the species). But if pregnancy will cause any kind of physical or mental health problems – such as where a marriage will be severely strained mentally, emotionally or financially – they can, of course use contraception.

Nonetheless, in these cases Judaism opposes the use of condoms for causing an artificial barrier between husband and wife, and it suggests the use of the pill or a diaphragm. Condoms are the ultimate barrier to intimacy. First, they serve as the ultimate spanner in the works of passion. A husband and wife are deep into foreplay, are panting and yearning for each other, when suddenly – STOP – there is a pause in the action. He withdraws from the bed to put on a condom. Is there anything less romantic than that?

Secondly, he is not in direct, intimate contact with the his wife's body, since a prophylactic now separates him from his wife. Of course, the main reason today for condoms is for singles having sex who fear the risk of disease, but more of premarital sex and its hazards later. Even so, large families are the norm in observant Jewish households. Children and family do enhance a couple's love for each and the beauty in holding a baby in one's arms is almost infinite (but more about this later on too).

Part Three

Sex for Single People

1. Do single people have more fun?

No chupa, no shtupa – no wedding, no bedding.   Yiddish proverb

A triumph of hope over experience
  Samuel Johnson, on the marriage of a widowed friend

Today, men and women meet for all kinds of reasons: fun, a cure for loneliness and boredom, sex, companionship, participation in the social circuit, and peer pressure. But one reason they almost invariably don't date for, until much later in life, is marriage. Statistics show that the average man or woman goes through six *serious* relationships before they end up marrying.

What this means is that they also break up at least six times before they finally commit. They will have endured harsh, and sometimes unbearable pain, at least six times before they settle down. Like a broken china dish that has been glued together after cracking, their heart has been broken and mended several times.

No one pays much attention to this, but the effects of this repeated loss of someone who is important to us are by no means minor. When Bonnie met Alex she was over the moon. She had previously seen Daniel for five years, and before splitting up she had lived with him for four of those years. But Daniel, a doctor, had begun another relationship with one of the nurses in the hospital and had abandoned Bonnie just when she thought he was going to propose. Bonnie told me that this time she wouldn't make the same mistake as before, and that she wouldn't trust Alex as much as she did her first lover.

'Daniel promised everything and delivered nothing. We were going to marry, buy an apartment together. In the end the only thing I have to show for our years together is that I don't really like myself. No man will ever do that to me again.' Alex broke up

with her seven months later as well, claiming that she was
impossible to please. Bonnie had been so hurt by a previous
relationship that she could no longer enter into a new relationship with the trust necessary to cement it into something
permanent.

Sexual loss

A few years ago I saw the movie *Total Recall* with a film-maker
friend of mine. While I marvelled at Arnold Schwarzenegger's
proficiency with a ray-gun, my friend claimed he was more impressed by the central premise of the plot. 'It's about memory
being the essence of human personality,' he said, 'Everything we
have experienced and learned, which is nothing but memory, is
what ultimately makes us what we are. You could alter a person
radically just by changing his memory.'

'I've often thought,' he continued, 'that when I meet the woman
of my dreams we should both have partial lobotomies.' I kept a
straight face, but asked him why.

'Because,' he said, 'then we could wipe out the memory of all
our old lovers, and love one another exclusively. Our potential for
complete intimacy would not be sullied by the past.'

Yet, this is exactly what happens today. By the time people get
married, there is this latent, lurking entanglement of premarital
sex. It would be simply unnatural not to feel exceedingly close to
someone after you have sex with them. But in premarital sex,
that is not meant to be. People consciously stifle the natural,
powerful emotions that should flow in the wake of sex. Commitment is the big 'C' word which is counteracted by that other 'c'
word: contraception.

Dealing with emotional loss

One of Judaism's key concerns is with bereavement because
bereavement leaves an indelible mark on us. When Virginia Kelly
died, her son, President Bill Clinton, had to leave immediately
after the funeral for a summit with President Yeltsin in Moscow.
He never gave himself a chance to digest the traumatic loss of a
mother he loved so dearly, and for months thereafter the press

commented on how drawn and down he looked. We can't shut off our hearts and expect it to give us no trouble, like a water tap.

Jewish law, therefore, stipulates that after a bereavement, God forbid, an individual must sit 'shiva', or seven days of mourning in which they don't fully participate in society and allow themselves to heal and slowly digest the emotional trauma. The full gamut of human emotions must be allowed to play themselves out if the individual is to recover from this terrible wound.

It is simply not natural to sustain the loss of a close relative and to be back at work two days later, smiling at colleagues and chatting with customers. Emotions require a healthy outlet, and Jewish law prescribes a legitimate emotional outlet for every human situation. Suppressing such a terrible loss will eventually have grave repercussions.

Similarly, it simply cannot be healthy for adults to consciously suppress the natural emotions which are born of sexual congress. This is no proper outlet for our emotions. It actually messes up our minds and our hearts when we suppress these automatic impulses and try to emerge from the encounter with no strings attached. The repeated disappointments and sharp pain of breaking up on many occasions with previous boyfriends or girlfriends snuffs out an essential part of us and we emerge hardened by our previous sexual experiences, when these should leave a soft and vulnerable memory.

Why it does not work

The problem is that we have simply experienced too much pain to trust anyone all that much. And this shows in marriage. Sure, we have the certificate and she is now known as Mrs so and so. But that doesn't change the simple fact that people marrying today are prone to hold back the deepest part of themselves in marriage to ensure that they never get hurt again.

It is a real problem that we are no longer getting as connected as people in the past, and are actively compromising our capacity to do so. And this to me is the strongest reason that divorce is so common today. From the start couples are not very strongly unified in the first place.

Single people should think seriously about these issues before they engage in every form of casual, commitment-free, and loveless sex. Marriage is taking the plunge. You see someone and after getting to know the essentials of the person in question – that they are nice, considerate, attractive, loving, have the right values, and are devoted to you – you leap into marriage. There is no guarantee that you will be happy or that the relationship will last. There never is.

But once you set your heart on the person in question, you jump into marriage – you allow yourself to fall. You place hope before your survival instinct. That is the essence of what makes us human. Marriage is a statement of the human love for companionship superseding our love for perfection. It really is quite irrational to put so much faith into someone who was once, and may yet again be, a stranger. But that's the beauty of marriage. It is a quintessential statement of faith from one human being to another. People who marry, and remain successfully married, are great optimists who somehow believe that love conquers all. They go into marriage expecting that there will be far more joyous occasions than painful ones. They really believe in the future and the person with whom they will share it.

But because of the path associated with lingering memories of broken relationships, people are not surrendering themselves fully into marriage. Rather, they very slowly and very cautiously surrender parts of themselves, incrementally. Therefore, when a problem crops up which in times gone by could never have severed a deeply married couple, the modern husband and wife find themselves torn apart, since their union was very tenuous in the first place.

2. Is marriage a mere symbol?

Here lies my wife, here let her lie. Now she's at peace, and so am I.
John Dryden, the epitaph for his wife

When a girl marries she exchanges the attention of many men for the inattention of one.   Helen Rowland

At the beginning of this book I discussed the modern phenomenon of emotionless, biological sex. Young couples will spend the night together and then awaken in the morning and feel barely that the other is in any way unique. They remain strangers. A man and a woman will date for four or five years, and still feel that they don't know each other.

Why marry?

A serious corollary of this lack of familiarity is the all-too-common phenomenon of some women, but especially men who refuse to commit to a woman in marriage, even when they have already been their girlfriends for many years. Alan and Charlotte had been dating at Oxford for more than two years. Both were highly intelligent, highly motivated British graduate students. Charlotte was two years older than Alan, and they started dating when she was thirty years old. After two years had elapsed, she began applying subtle pressure on Alan to commit. But, though she felt her biological clock was ticking, he was still relatively young, much too young to marry in his opinion at any rate.

They were living together, and Charlotte approached me for advice about the situation. 'Give him an ultimatum,' I said.

'But I'm afraid. What if he decides to leave me. I'm sure that I will never love someone this much again.' 'If he doesn't want to marry you,' I replied, 'then even right now he isn't really yours. You have to show him that you're not desperate.' 'But I am desperate. Of course I know that I shouldn't show him that. But I can't help it. I don't know what to do without him.'

'Well, at the very least,' I said, 'you should stop living together. Show him that you're serious. If you live together and he gets everything he wants without commitment, why should he agree to sign the contract you're giving him. What possible benefit can there be.' Charlotte ignored my advice and six months later the relationship fizzled out because of the tension.

Putting a value on marriage

If I had one pound for each woman who has complained to me that they cannot get their boyfriends to ask the big question, or at least commit to seriously exploring the possibility of marriage, I could have been Bill Gates by now (and who would then need to write books on sex?).

There are many reasons for the dread of marriage, not least of which are the awesome financial and social consequences of the decision. But the problem in an age where most couples live and sleep together before marriage, is that there no longer is any clear reason why people should marry. What advantage is there to be had? He has a warm body next to him at night, someone to look after the home. And she in turn has a man in her life who loves her and makes her laugh. What need then is there for a formal ceremony?

Sometimes I wonder whether women really understand what their agreement in the sixties to commitment-free sex did for them. It just ensured that now that men could get sex readily and without strings attached, they had no good reason to marry and commit. As one attractive twenty-nine year-old woman who had just broken up with a long-standing boyfriend said to me, 'If we women all agreed together not to give any man sex outside of marriage, they'd all be lining up at the altar!'

A close friend flew in from Miami to discuss with me how unhappy she was. She had been living with her boyfriend for four years already, even though he had promised that they would marry after two. Moreover, in spite of having a very good job with a high income, he would sit there with a calculator at the end of each month and tell her how much she owed him, charging her fifty percent of every expense, and conveniently disregarding the fact that she cleaned the entire apartment and made him dinner every night. On top of it all, she was a highly attractive woman with an excellent career of her own. And he still wouldn't marry her.

'Are you crazy?' I asked her. 'Why are you selling yourself so cheap?'

She really had no response to the question. Like Charlotte, she had agreed to move in and now all of a sudden felt hemmed in. She felt that having invested so much into this relationship, she didn't want to risk destroying it. And so she allowed it to destroy herself instead.

Women today have simply forgotten what true love is and what a real compliment is. A guy will tell a girl that he loves her and that he wants to share his life with her, that she is beautiful and that he cannot live without her. She is very impressed and flattered. So she saddles up her stuff and brings it around to his place. But, there is only one compliment that a man can give a woman: 'Will you be my wife.'

It is the ultimate compliment, because it comes with a price that he is prepared to pay. All other compliments are just words. When he says those words he is not just thinking about sex, but about a future of you and him together. By offering marriage, he embraces the choice to give up choice, sacrificing and forswearing the possibility of romance with another woman for all time to come.

Is marriage really 'only' a symbol?

We understand the necessity of symbols and their importance. And yet, suddenly, when it comes to marriage, people say it is 'only' a symbol. I once gave a lecture on the subject of why people should convert relationships into marriage. A couple who had been living together for twenty seven years, but who had never married each other, came along. Now, no one could say that they were not committed to each other. In his will everything he had was being left to his 'partner.' But he refused to get married, because he had had a bad marriage and he felt that marriage was unworkable.

'Marriage,' he told me, 'is nothing more than a piece of paper, a sign to the community, and our love for each other is far greater than any symbol. Reducing our commitment to each other to a badge would just degrade the special quality of our relationship. Symbols just aren't important.'

I disagreed. Even if it were true that marriage is only a symbol, symbols are highly important. Every company needs a logo, and indeed vast sums of money are spent on this. Every country has a flag, and every religion needs icons of what its faith represents. For a Jew, for example, wearing a 'yarmulke' (head covering: 'yoreh malkah' – I fear the King) is a statement of pride in one's identity. We might even say that symbols are what life is all about. A graduate student would not be pleased if after four years of work his D.Phil was refused 'because it is unimportant.'

Marriage means clarity

Although a symbol might indeed be construed as a mere two-dimensional representation, our willingness to embrace or reject that symbol is, in fact, the weathervane for what we feel toward the object it represents. Visual images make their impact by stamping their imprint on the observer. For example if I sat and described all of the details of the house where I grew up in Florida, every reader would have a different picture of what the house looked like in their mind, because everyone has their own interpretation. But, if I were to print the picture alongside this paragraph of what the house looks like, every reader would know exactly what it looks like and have the exact same image

When a man wears a wedding ring it is a statement to the outside world that not only is he in love with someone, but that he is proud of his commitment. So proud is he that he firmly and daily announces to the world that he belongs to someone. He has no hesitation in removing himself from intimate forms of affection from other women. And, when a woman proudly displays her wedding ring, she is announcing to all who wish to hear that she believes her fiancée is special and considers herself lucky. Both see the positive side of commitment, and want others to see it too. Most importantly, it conveys to everyone else exactly how much they mean to each other.

Conveying what cannot be expressed

'Living together' on the other hand means vastly different things to different people. You may, for instance, live together but still agree to date other people. One hundred different people will have a hundred different interpretations as to what your commitment to each other means, once they hear that it is only a relationship. But if they stand at your wedding and witness your marriage, everyone understands exactly what you mean to each other.

But marriage means the same thing for all people. It connotes the exclusivity of sex, the commitment to build a home and raise a family, and to put each other first always. Surely, when people are living together, one may ask one of the participants if the relationship is serious. But to ask that of two people who are married to each other would be ludicrous. You don't need to tell people, 'We have it all, we're living together, I love you, you're mine, we go out together, and we share the same bed, the same money.'

In a Jewish marriage this is powerfully expressed, as the bride and groom stand under the wedding canopy, the bride wears no jewellery and the groom has nothing in his pockets. The bride also wears a veil to symbolise that irrespective of her beauty and irrespective of their financial status – even if their pockets are empty – they still love each other and commit in marriage. Their commitment to each other is independent of external considerations. This visual representation of their love is something that 'relationship' could never convey without further explanation.

Finances

The fact, however, that marriage is a perfect expression of love does not mean that married people can take it for granted. They must try and live up to the symbol as well before they decide to get married. And this can be tough. Jane knew that she was marrying into a very wealthy family. But she didn't know that she would be asked to sign a prenuptial agreement, and she certainly didn't expect to be asked to do so on the night before her wedding. But the written contract was presented to her as a *fait accompli* by the family's lawyer and as a condition for her fiancé proceeding with the marriage on the following afternoon.

With no choice left to her, she signed it with tears in her eyes. But the feeling of humiliation never left her and she never really bonded with her new husband. They divorced seven months later. 'Money was never an issue for me,' she told me, 'so why did Robert make it an issue by having me sign that silly piece of paper. If he was concerned that I was marrying him only for his money, then he shouldn't be marrying me at all. But you can't have it both ways. You can't pretend that money is not an issue, and then make it all or nothing problem the night before the wedding.'

Let's face it. Money is incredibly important to people. I can't begin to enumerate how many couples I have seen who have witnessed the steady deterioration of their marriage because they did not share a joint bank account, or where they had prenuptial agreements, or they just kept their earnings to themselves. Often these people are hedging their bets. You are not sure if it will work out and so you minimise your areas of co-operation. However, when you hedge your bets you are not channelling all your efforts into making it a success.

In effect you are saying, 'Everything I have, my prosperity and my future, my clothes, food and house is bought with my money, but I am not sharing it with you.' This unwillingness to become one flesh is particularly a problem for couples who do not have children yet, as it leaves a small crevice which later might grow into a wide open space. Marriage is a statement of total commitment, and it is undermined when external factors are allowed to serve as a barrier to a couple uniting fully. Therefore, even couples who are about to marry should resist the temptation not to trust their intended spouse totally. Even in the most insignificant way they must strive to be described as being one. (And the same is true of sharing the same surname. I know of many women who object to patriarchy within society and refuse to take their husband's last name. 'Fine,' I tell them. 'So let him take your last name, or have a hybrid last name. One way or another, even in name you should be united!)

3. Career or marriage?

Men should keep their eyes wide open before marriage, and half-shut afterwards.
                                                    Madeleine de Scudery

A man in love is incomplete until he has married. Then he is finished.
                                                    Zsa Zsa Gabor

When I first came to Oxford, I was under the impression that I would be spending most of my time teaching Judaism. That seemed to go with the profession of being a Rabbi. In reality, however, the most common subject which comes up today in my conversation with students are their problems with relationships. But, I am no longer amazed that modern-day relationships, which really should be the greatest source of joy in a person's life, usually become the greatest source of pain and agony. For, in my experience, the overriding factor in the fragility of today's relationships is an inability to reconcile the conflict between wanting to be loved and doing everything possible to avoid commitment. What happens today is that, from an early age, we start inventing our own rules and expectations, and are then surprised when things don't quite work out.

Commitment no longer has a shared meaning

A girl who was very close to our children and would kindly volunteer to baby-sit for us, always complained about how her boyfriend was not sufficiently committed to her. She would lament that he refused to devote a sufficient amount of time to her, and would always put his academic work before her. Eventually, the problem, or her perception of it, became so acute that she decided to call it quits and broke the relationship off. I was quite fond of her boyfriend and the break-up surprised me. I suggested to her that perhaps she had treated him unfairly, even hypocritically. She made an expression of disbelief. 'How so?' she wanted to know.

'Well, let's say he had turned around to you last week, before you broke up, and said, 'Let's get married.' Would you have agreed?' Without even hesitating she said, 'Of course not. I am much too young to get married.'

That was exactly what I expected to hear. 'Well,' I said, 'in that case you were as undevoted to him as he was to you. In the same way you complain that he wasn't prepared to commit himself sufficiently to you, and this bothered you enough to break it off, you are no different. You are also as yet unprepared to make a substantial commitment.'

This is the common problem of all teenagers today. The constraints imposed by today's relationships present many young people with an impossible dilemma. Everything inside them says: find someone to love you. But everything outside them barks: You have to be nuts to get married. It is commitment they feel and commitment they desire. But they can't do anything about it. This girl wanted to be loved, so much so that she could never get enough of her boyfriend of whom she was very fond. On the other hand, it had been inculcated in her that she was not to get married before a certain age, or at the very least, before she had finished her degree.

On the rare occasion at Oxford that two students announce their intention to marry, their friends express not joy and support for the decision, but confusion and, sometimes, undisguised hostility. 'Was she pregnant?' 'No, she wasn't.' 'But they're probably very religious?' One close friend of mine, a law student, who

became engaged to be married at twenty three years old, came to
me virtually in tears when he told his best friend that he was
getting married, and the friend told him he was 'crazy.'

Personal success, a lost continent

Never in history was there a more goal-oriented society than our
own. As a Rabbi to students at a leading university, I can personally attest to the naked ambition of the students, from every
social and religious background. Our parents push us to make our
lives a success and everyone today wants to be something important. And, of course, there's nothing wrong with that. Any responsible parent would teach their children nothing less.

But a common modern-day scenario is that an ambitious young
woman will go to a good University and fall in love with a
romantic young man who is equally purposeful. When she comes
home to tell her mother that she wants to get married, instead of
a look of joy, her mother too gives her a look of concern. 'Don't do
what I did. I made the mistake of getting married early and I
never did what I really wanted to in life.' She might encourage
her to marry someone in the not too distant future, but she will
also instil within her a sense of priorities. There is no reason to
put off promising career prospects. Marriage can wait.

And so, at every stage in our early life we are taught to make
something of ourselves, at the expense of anything else, even
those things which are most natural and necessary. We are
taught to believe that if we marry young and have children, we
will never realise our professional aspirations. Success means
money, a degree from a good university and landing a good job.
We glorify football players and Hollywood movie stars as role-
models when we read of their high salaries and we envy their
'success.' The fact that so many of them are divorced, or on their
third marriage, or live their lives in complete disarray does not
affect our judging them to be a success.

Yet, if we stand back and think it seems incredible that in
society today success is measured in this way. A man who works
his whole life as a car mechanic, eking out a living at £200 a week,
but who is a loving husband and a great father, gets no respect at
all in society because he wasn't ambitious enough. But, if someone rises to be Chairman of IBM, is thrice divorced and has

children who refuse to speak with them, is he to be considered a success? Are we really that convinced of our personal mediocrity that only our professional pursuits count?

What comes natural?

Have we forgotten that when we inculcate upon our child the idea that at all costs he or she must be a success, the child may not understand that this should also mean success in one's personal affairs? Aren't we aiding and abetting these problems which our children will experience in the future?

If a young man or woman does not learn to prioritise family life before their professional life prior to marriage, they will not do so even after marriage. In his book *Why Men Are the Way They Are?*, psychologist Warren Farrell points out that what makes a man a success in the marketplace often makes him a disaster at home: 'Men try to make themselves attractive to women by the very process that ultimately alienates them from women.' He works hard to make a lot of money in order to become more desirable to attractive women who have many options. But then he marries. Working hard is now what he does for a living, and he neglects his family and his wife. The more he neglects his wife, the more bitter and acerbic she becomes to him. He now seeks to release himself of the pressure of his life in the company of women in his office where psychologist, Carol Botwin cites in *Tempted Women*, 74 per cent of all extramarital dalliances begin.

If you didn't learn to get your priorities straight as a student, then you will always put your career first. Suppose your wife always hears you talk about the attractive woman you work with whole days and long working nights, you will see your wife's protestations as absurd jealousy at best, and harmful paranoia at worst. 'That's work honey.' But in fact, aside from the important question of when a husband or wife can reasonably ask their spouse to keep away from another man or woman out of legitimate jealousy, this issue revolves around the question of what comes first. If you believe that marriage precedes money-making, then you will at the very least seek to address your wife's objections seriously and take the necessary precautions.

Growing up

At Oxford I notice in particular how, on the whole, the students arrive far more interested in sex than love. This is especially true of the male students. Almost every young man I know at Oxford can tell you exactly how many women he has slept with at the drop of a hat. Only last week a twenty-two-year-old friend told me that the woman with whom he spent the night before was number eleven. By the same token, however, I notice that every mature adult eventually begins to feel incomplete. We gradually become dissatisfied with diplomas and professional promotion. We crave someone to share with the depths of not doing well on exams or being rejected from a job application. Exciting one-night stands they may be, but they no longer fill this void.

I remember how lonely I felt during my Rabbinical student years. I had left home to go to a boarding school 3000 miles away, and whenever I saw couples travelling together on an aeroplane, I envied them. Wherever they travelled, they were together. I remember thinking to myself that when a man travels with his wife, wherever he goes his home travels with him. These couples were never alone. But I was always alone. First getting attached to my peers at school and, as a student, the extended family atmosphere of friends from all over the country. But then going home to visit and getting attached to my real family. I felt like a yo-yo.

We must take these feelings of incompleteness seriously. We must all ask ourselves an honest question: does being a good parent, a good spouse, a good friend and a good human being figure into our definition of success as much as professional or financial success? And if so, are we presently undertaking the necessary steps to ensure that we will indeed succeed in those areas? A woman was living with a man who promised to get engaged by June 1. The date came and went. She was very unhappy. 'Why don't you keep him to his word?', I asked.

'Well,' she said 'he just lost his job, and it's not fair to push him on the marriage issue right now. It's the wrong time.' 'Wrong time?,' I asked. 'This is the perfect time. It's specifically when he is low and sees how nasty the world can be that he must turn to someone who will never abandon him. The real desire for marriage results from our recognition of each other's vulnerability.'

A year ago, the stock market fluctuations sunk many of my friends into a deep depression as they watched their net worth sink by five and ten per cent in a single day. I asked them whether they felt as depressed the day that they fell out with one of their ten closest friends, thus decreasing their intimate friendships by ten percent as well? We must learn to redefine our success first and foremost in terms of our personal lives. Only then do we truly stand a chance of finding fulfilment and happiness, and being able to cope with its set-backs in a mature and stable way.

4. Holding out for the best

No man should marry until he has studied anatomy and dissected at least one woman.
Honoré de Balzac, *Physiologie du marriage*, 1829

Wouldn't it be wise to wait until you are pregnant?   Anonymous

An Israeli friend of mine had been highly promiscuous throughout his life and had never endured a long-term relationship. Then, for the first time he met a wonderful woman and they dated for two years, two years longer than he had been involved with anyone else. At this point I began receiving calls from him telling me how bored he was with her. 'She is a great girl,' he said, 'but she isn't adventurous enough.'

A month later he had broken off the relationship. He next saw her with another man on a date, standing outside a bar. He was so unnerved by this sight, and so overcome with jealousy, that he drove his car straight into a traffic light. In a later conversation he told me that he thought he did this subconsciously to get her attention. She came running over to him crying and abandoning her date in the process to check that he was not hurt. This brought them back together again for another half year, but then it was back to the same complaint that he was bored. He left her again, this time claiming it was for good.

When he came to visit me in England a short time later, he made disparaging remarks about her intelligence and her dull personality. But whenever I suggested I agreed with him, he quickly shut me up. He refused to hear any criticism about her, defending her to the hilt on any point. 'In fact,' he said, 'she is a wonderful woman, though not as experienced as some of the other girls I have known' – he once told me 'All she does is lie there in bed. I have to take the initiative.'

I at first thought that my remarks upset him because he was feeling bad about the thought that he might have hurt her. But then it struck me that indeed he was in love with her. I piped up one day and told him, 'I bet that this is the woman that you are going to marry.' He responded, 'I hope not. If I do, I can look forward to a life of stultifying boredom. But you are probably right, I think I will end up marrying her.' And so it was, just a year later.

God's own gift to women

Men do have this terrible fear of dedicating themselves to one particular relationship, one of the foremost causes of which is a falsely inflated opinion of themselves. They have this uncanny knack of believing that every woman in every situation is interested in them. On top of this, many young (and some not so young) men feel that by taking themselves off the market they will be depriving hundreds of women who would otherwise be interested in them. It is therefore almost an act of cruelty for them to pledge allegiance to one woman. What will be with all the others who want them as well?

At Oxford I hear their refrains all the time. 'Did you see the way that waitress handed me my change in the restaurant. I could tell she wanted me.' 'You know Melody who lives across the hall from me? Well, although she has never even said hello to me, and often crosses herself when she passes by my room and throws salt over her back, I can tell from the way she walked by my room last week and dropped her key that she gets weak at the knees whenever she thinks of me. She just can't wait to have me.' 'Did you hear how that air hostess asked me if I want milk and sugar? But then, I do that to all women.' I see this kind of arrogance in many of the young unmarried men (and women) that I know.

Crossing the Rubicon

If a man felt, however, that he was lucky to have the affections of even one woman – that she still loved him – notwithstanding the fact that he had faults and could at times be inconsiderate, selfish, and angry – then he would feel privileged that anyone at all has agreed to marry him. It is humility that allows us to share a healthy relationship with another human being and arrogance that makes it impossible to commit. Marriage is the biggest decision of our lives, and we therefore often feel paralysed in making a choice. But, the beginning of making the correct decision is to understand what prevents us from making the decision in the first place.

At twenty one I too was terrorised by the thought of commitment. I found myself dating a wonderful girl, and although I liked her very much, after the second week I did a lot of soul-searching. Hasidic Jews date to marry and therefore tend to marry early, but I decided that there was no way that I could possibly marry at such a young age. The fear of limiting my horizons and possibilities grabbed hold of me and made me shudder. But, I didn't know how to break this to her.

The next day I picked her up and took her for a car ride around Miami Beach. We had a wonderful time. Nevertheless, the end of this great day turned sad when I finally broke the news to her that after careful consideration I had decided that I was too young to marry. My wife-to-be just stared at me in disbelief as if I had been misleading her all along. Why had I been wasting her time? I quickly added that it was no reflection on her, and that in two years time I would be very happy to marry someone as lovely as her, but she just stared ahead, avoiding my gaze. I asked her if she would wait for me, and she told me that she was not sure.

This surprised me. I had (have?) a very inflated opinion of myself and expected her response to be that she would cross oceans and rivers for me, and was prepared to lay down her life to have me. As it happened, she finally looked at me and said, 'You seem pretty confused and therefore I don't think I would wait. What impressed me most about you was the maturity that I thought you possessed beyond your years. However, it now seems that I was mistaken.' She turned and walked away from me and I saw that her eyes were red. All at once I was confronted with a powerful decision.

I knew that my complaints were merely of my own making. I imagined two things. First, how would I feel if I heard that she had become engaged to someone else? I decided that I would be deeply hurt. In fact, I thought that I would never be able to get over it. Second, I was definitely feeling lower than an anthill at that moment. I felt that I had been deceitful and that my lack of straightforwardness was hurting another human being severely. But this was absurd. Should I marry someone merely because I felt sorry for her and did not want to hurt her? Or was it absurd? Did this mean I loved her? I decided that it did. I just couldn't bear to watch her in pain. She had already begun to mean something very important to me.

Cold feet

But even after our engagement I was plagued by doubts whether I was making the right choice – and I feel very deeply for all those who suffer its effects as well. A great many people spend what should be one of the most beautiful periods of their lives – their engagements – wondering if they are doing the right thing. Guests are beginning to respond, the caterer has his deposit, the hall is paid for, and the tailor is making final touches on the wedding dress. Suddenly, bingo! 'Is he really the right guy?' 'Is she the right girl?' You were sure that this was the person that you wanted to marry. So sure, in fact, that you put a huge amount of time and money into the marriage arrangements, not to mention showing off your fiancé(e) to all your family and friends and speaking about them in glowing terms. What is going wrong?

The explanation is that suddenly the enormity of the decision hits us. This, after all, is the first face that we will be seeing upon awakening, the last face upon going to sleep, the person we will go on holiday with, the one that we will laugh and cry and hurl with, that must be entertaining and stimulating enough to preserve us for the rest of our lives, our only sexual partner (at least in theory), and so on. It is, therefore, totally natural and can be easily overcome. At least, so long as we understand that when you suddenly find massive fault at the time you are meant to commit to someone whom love, your complaints have no real substance and arise entirely from the natural human fear of taking the pledge.

Although Judaism is a non-proselytising religion, many non-Jewish students approach me every year at Oxford saying that they want to convert to Judaism. The conversion is a long and arduous process that usually lasts about two years and involves intensive study and a commitment to a Jewish observant life-style. About 60 per cent of those who begin the process usually end up dropping out. I usually know which ones will do so. When I'm approached by a conversion candidate, I always ask them why they want to convert? Those who give me strong, rational, well-considered reasons – 'I believe that the Jews are the chosen people, I like Jewish tradition and kosher food,' 'I want to reverse the discrimination that Jews have suffered throughout the ages,' 'I'm in love with a Jewish guy or girl' – are almost always the ones who end up dropping out. But those who cannot give a reason, who just say 'I don't quite know why I want to be Jewish. I've just felt this way,' they are the ones who almost always end up persevering through the entire process and becoming Jewish.

Engagement and marriage are similar to this. You've got to take the plunge, particularly if you're young. Because it is such a big decision, if you sit and scrutinise every last detail, you will no doubt drive yourself mad. And so, the only memories of the days prior to your marriage will be memories that you would much rather forget. Focus instead on the big things, the principal considerations, that should go into choosing a spouse. Marriage is only partly rational.

Marrying later in life

The relationships guru John Gray recently disputed in his book *Mars and Venus on a Date*, that the rising age of marriage is a cause of concern. 'Really, it is a sign of greater wisdom in young couples. They are waiting to get married. They are wanting to first get a sense of who they are...' But where is this greater wisdom being demonstrated? In the rising rate of divorce? Pre-nuptial experimentation has not led to happier or more stable marriages. In the UK, the number of divorces increased six-fold between 1961 and 1990.

Why should we be concerned at the vastly rising national age for marriage? If people eventually marry anyway, what is the difference? One answer, of course, is that it can cause much harm to wait. When we are young but wait, we will no doubt encounter someone who would have made a perfect marriage partner but who is no longer available when we are finally ready to make up our mind. I always tell my students that it is far better to marry the right person at the wrong time, then the wrong person at the right time.

Secondly, when people marry younger they can grow together in a way that fully formed adults cannot. As we are older we also become far more set in our ways and we find it more difficult to compromise and build our lives around somebody else. It is far more difficult to learn from, and share a life with, a stranger who comes into our lives. Furthermore, the later we marry the less children we are bound to have, which certainly for ethnic populations like the Jews is imperative. The Jewish birth-rate today is so low that studies predict that by the year 2035 the current world Jewish population of fourteen million will be down to five or six million souls.

I have often been told that the last revenge of married people is to inflict the same agony on those who are blissfully single. Indeed, the world today is incredibly cynical about marriage. But, I write these lines not in the hope that you who are single will forfeit your privileged status and remove the temptation from those of us who have taken the marital plunge. But rather, in an attempt to help identify what it is we really seek from our relationships. I am convinced that a man or woman who find stability and passion early in life will not have to choose between career and relationship. On the contrary, having been fortified with the unconditional love of a permanent partner, they will be untouchable and impregnable to the rat-race of the world, and succeed vastly in their professional ambitions.

5. Choosing a spouse

And he said, O Lord, the God of my master Abraham, I pray you send me good speed this day ... And let it come to pass that the maiden to whom I shall say 'Let down your pitcher, I pray you, that I may drink,' and she shall say, 'Drink, and to your camels also will I give drink,' be the one You have appointed for your servant Isaac.
Genesis 24: verse 12-13, Eliezer praying that God send him a prospective bride for Isaac

Courtship is the time during which the girl decides whether or not she can do any better.
Anonymous

In a remote area, according to primitive custom, a man would buy
his bride from her father for a number of cows. Obviously, the
worth of the woman was gauged by the number of cows she would
fetch. There was a young woman who was considered plain at
best, and her father despaired of getting more than two cows for
her. One day a young man came and asked for her hand in
marriage. The father was amazed when the man offered ten cows
for her. He insisted on paying this exorbitant sum, even though
the father was willing to take much less. The young couple
married of course.

Some time later the father visited his daughter and son-in-law.
He was amazed to find how his daughter had changed. She looked
radiant – beautiful, even. He remarked on this difference and she
explained as follows: 'Father, for years I was told I was plain. I
believed it, and it became true. However, my husband told me
otherwise. He saw me as someone beautiful, and was willing to
demonstrate it. He told me that in his estimation, I was a ten-cow
woman. And thanks to him, I became a ten-cow woman.'

Consumer values

In the West, and especially in the United States, we have forgotten this simple truth. We all search for the best. We want the best
Sony Walkman, the latest BMW sports car, the most expensive
Versace suit, and an expensive house with as many amenities as
possible – swimming pool, sauna, tennis courts – in fact we want
it all, now.

There is nothing wrong with this in itself. It is in fact something which is implicit in having abundant choice between objects
which function in a one-dimensional way. It is very easy to set two
cellular telephones on a scale, match their features and warran-
ties, and decide which one is superior to the other, which one is
the best.

We run into problems, however, if we apply the 'best' to human
beings. I was sitting with a friend who came from a poor family
and, through his own efforts entirely, became wealthy. He was
thirty four years old and still not married. I asked him why. 'Well
Shmuley,' he told me with a sigh, 'I have dated so many women.
Beautiful women, smart women, but none of them has been right.

I don't know. I'm not just going to marry anyone yet. I am going to marry someone very special. The best. I believe I deserve it.'

'Of course you deserve the best,' I said. 'Everyone does. But you have to stop treating dating a woman like a business acquisition. How can you connect with a woman if you see her as a trophy and ignore her depth as a human being?' In relationships, there is no such thing as 'the best.' The woman to whom you are attracted, who is loving to you, and whom you respect, who shares your values, and is willing to spend her life with you, is the best because she is everything you are looking for. But the moment you begin to compare her qualities with fifty other women, you'll just begin to drive yourself crazy.'

The way in which we look at marriage today is, in fact, the way in which royal marriages of old were conducted. They were decided not on love or attraction. Rather, they were determined entirely on paper. The woman whose father was the more celebrated prince, who could bring the largest dowry, and with whose kingdom a strategic alliance was most beneficial, was chosen as the bride for the crown prince of the land. Today young men and women are doing exactly the same thing. They date and marry other men and women based on their education, job, financial resources, looks, and future ambitions. Whether or not this person best accords with what they are looking for most in a relationship, and whether or not they are able to fill the hole at the centre of our being, rarely matters. Indeed studies show that 94 per cent of all American university graduates will only date someone who also has a university degree. And 97 per cent of women who earn $50,000 per year will only date a man in a similar or higher earning bracket.

But it just doesn't work. Hollywood is filled with beautiful husbands and wives who are married, yet they cheat on each other constantly and divorce even more rapidly. Now, why? These are the most beautiful people in the world. Why would they feel the need to find someone else? A guy who is married to a world-famous actress that so many other men will kill for, has surely married 'the best.' So why does he ditch her in favour of someone else? It means that even if you are married to the most beautiful woman in the world (and this is the reason why you got married in the first place) she simply cannot possibly contain all the qualities of ten other attractive women.

Goodness is what counts in marriage

When we apply consumer terminology to describe a human relationship we are making a mistake. If your criterium is 'the best', you will end up never finding it but rather skipping from bed to bed. Human beings are multifaceted and human life is infinitely deep. We remove people's unique and infinite spiritual character and reduce them to mere tissue when we sit down and compare them to one another like a kitchen appliance. The only thing that can bring real warmth and love into our lives is another human being who is not merely skin, flesh and bones. We must connect to our spouse in a deep and personal way. External, aesthetic attraction is the bait, but love is specific. When a man wants sex he can obtain it from virtually any woman. But once he falls in love, no other woman can serve as a substitute for her. Only his beloved will do.

What is central, therefore, with regard to the person who we are considering for marriage is the question of goodness. Because goodness is a measure, not of what fleshy qualities a person possesses, such as playing the piano, but rather of how fully a person has developed and brought to the fore their infinite spiritual potential. Tammy was a young woman who had tragically been widowed while still in her twenties. She was desperate and alone until she met Max, who quickly became the light of her life. He was successful in business and lavished her with gifts and impressed her with his caring attitude. She was so happy that after seven months of dating, she was hopelessly in love and was flattered to receive his proposal for marriage.

But shortly after they married, she discovered that her husband was completely dishonest in business. Every day people would call his office and home to be paid for outstanding bills. He had not informed her that he had twice declared bankruptcy under suspicious circumstances. He would invariably lie to his wife and his creditors about his finances. And although this did not directly affect his wife and he always remained generous and gracious to her, their marriage fell apart because she lost respect for him. They began to keep separate bedrooms. I went to see Tammy and asked if there was any hope of a reconciliation. She was very blunt. 'I cannot live with a man who is so dishonest. I feel dirty every time I am with him, and I want to be clean.' I wondered whether she was right, for Max obviously loved her. But, once respect is lost in marriage, loss of love is sure to follow.

What matters is a willingness to learn

In another instance where I was asked to mediate, Gabi came to see me very late one night in tears. She and Simon had been dating for nearly four years. They loved each other very much and Simon desperately wanted to get married, but Gabi hesitated. That night they had gone out to dinner and had an argument, and Simon severely lost his temper at Gabi and yelled at her. 'He frightens me. I love him and I'd like to spend the rest of my life with him. But I'm afraid of him.' Simon acknowledged his bad temper and realised it was destroying his life. He went to therapy for it and tried his best to change. He wrote many letters to Gabi begging her forgiveness and pledging every effort toward becoming a better person. But none of this helped. Gabi broke off the relationship.

I went to see her and told her that she should give him a chance. 'If he continues with his outbursts, then break it off. But now he's really trying.' She would, however, have none of it. 'I was raised in a home,' she told me, 'where I don't remember my parents having even one argument. The fact that Simon and I fight just shows that we're not right for each other.' I told her that her parents were very fortunate, but their experience was hardly the norm. Many times since she has questioned whether or not she did the right thing, or whether she should have worked with him to overcome his anger.

I am convinced Gabi's stubbornness is a common fault. Simon was different in that he openly acknowledged his shortcomings and in that respect he was a good person who was committed to change. What we, like her, fail to consider carefully is that when it comes to human beings and potential marital partners, there is no such thing as a person without any flaws. The only thing that matters is that we should know exactly what *our* special needs and concerns are, within reason, of course, when we enter into a relationship. As long as the person we are dating satisfies those needs, then they are perfect for us. Even if in the department of material, aesthetic, or intellectual gifts they cannot compare with the ideal that we have entertained throughout our life, this is still true. A warm and loving human being is much better than an abstraction in any circumstance.

Discovering our irreducible essence

Every man and woman has a single inner point that best captures their essence. For me, the defining point of my life was my parent's divorce, and the concomitant desire to heal the world. Therefore, the great challenge for me, and what drives everything I do, is the need to make things fit. I know that I am broken at the core of my being, and therefore I strive to make people get along, and to restore hope to people like myself whose life experiences have told them to give up. This is my personal therapy and what brings me healing.

Therefore, what I needed in a spouse above all else was someone who first could understand and forgive my considerable imperfection, and second, someone who could give me infinite support in my darker moments of self-questioning and doubt. In short, I needed a very feminine woman – someone incredibly nurturing, loving, and forgiving and someone who didn't mind playing second fiddle to a husband who often needs to be in the spotlight.

But this is not true, obviously, for everyone. A close friend of mine was the exact opposite. He came from a very loving and prosperous family, which, to an extent, impeded his ambition. He was whole at his core, so he never really worked hard at school or in University. Not being unhappy or doubting his self-worth, he never felt the need to substantiate himself or gain the acclamation of others. When he married, therefore, he married someone not as nurturing, but rather more pushy and slightly more masculine. Someone who would coerce him to maximise his potential.

I firmly believe that this is what we should look for, someone who fulfils the one central component of our lives which is most lacking. While there may not necessarily be many people who currently embody a limitless capacity for goodness, love and selflessness, there does exist a tremendous bank of people who possess internal goodness that must be brought to the fore, and marriage helps us translate our virtue and promise from potential to the actual. Marriage is a supreme educational tool which can be utilised to teach people how to put someone else first.

Finished products, people whose potential for goodness is already fully manifest, have little left to learn. If Simon were perfect, what valuable contribution could Gabi make to his life? Why would he need her? More than loving her, he really needed her, but she was blind to the possibility presented to her.

In the Book of Proverbs King Solomon says that 'As in water face answers face, so does the heart of man answer man'– whatever emotion you extend to someone will be returned. When you look upon your spouse and actually treat them like they are the best, then they become the best. When you show them extraordinary love and cherish them as the world's greatest treasure, then they will dress, look, and feel like a million bucks, because that's how you make them feel. But if you approach your spouse with constant evaluation, or worse, with doubt, as if you're not sure that you made the right decision, then your doubts will become a self-fulfilling prophecy. Your husband or wife will begin to feel, look, and act like somewhat inadequate, such is their misery when married to someone who is dissatisfied with them.

The choice to make the effort is ours.

6. What if you drive each other crazy?

We sleep in separate rooms, we have dinner apart, we take separate vacations – we're doing everything we can to keep our marriage together.
                                                    Rodney Dangerfield

The first lie detector was made out of the rib of a man. And they have been unable to improve on that model ever since.
                                                    Anonymous

Countless loving couples break up because of practical differences. I watch it happen all the time. When they fight they are broken-hearted because they hate being estranged from one another. But they can't stop arguing. Love, as they say, gives you wings, and allows you to surmount every hurdle that lies between you and your beloved. Yet, isn't it astonishing then that this same love is so often blighted by differences in practical living?

Jack was a student who studied philosophy at Oxford a number of years ago. He got a good job in London following his graduation. In his second year at work he met Barbara, an attractive young woman and dated her seriously. After six months he was sure that this was the one he wanted to marry and, having been extremely impressed at how much they loved each other, I encouraged him to take the big plunge. They got engaged and asked me to perform the wedding in one year's time.

Nonetheless, about a month later, severe problems developed and they fought like cats and dogs. They thought of calling off the wedding. But because they loved each other they decided they were going to live together to see if they could make things work. 'Better find out now than later' was their attitude. I advised against 'test-driving' the relationship. I explained to them my position, that when a couple have married and are stuck in the same boat, they strive to make the marriage work. But that if you are just living together, the first time a major difficulty crops up, you throw in the towel. The attitude becomes, Who needs this? And the love you feel for each other won't be enough to surmount your difficulties.

They did not heed my advice, and began their experiment. It started out OK until they reached an apparently insurmountable obstacle. Barbara came from a comfortable family. As such, her every desire had always been provided, and although she was not stuck-up or spoiled, she was not nearly as motivated as Jack. Moreover, hers was a loving background, two parents with a wonderful marriage who always put their children first. Jack, on the other hand, had lost his father at an early age and was riddled with insecurities. He felt he had to prove himself always. He believed in hard work, and felt that his fiancée was lazy. After time, he began to see her as a parasite. Barbara was not working and he would call her at eleven am and she would still be asleep.

Gradually, this led him to lose respect for her. Although he himself was charitable, he still could not live with someone who seemed to him to be a charity case herself. He decided to break the engagement off. Barbara returned to her parents in Manchester the very next morning, and he called me in anger. 'You're wrong Shmuley for trying to bring people together who are incompatible. I love Barbara, but I don't like her. So I can't live with her.' He went back to his busy and ambitious life. But within a few weeks he had sunk into a deep melancholy, and his work suffered terribly, especially after he heard that Barbara had become engaged to another man. He couldn't stop thinking and speaking about her.

Nevertheless, he maintained 'I still believe I made the right decision. It would never have worked out.' A year later I happened to publish an essay which argued that since men and women come from different, often contradictory worlds, it is impossible to comprehend every aspect of our spouse, and so at times it is important just to accommodate the will of our partners in life, notwithstanding our lack of comprehension or appreciation of those aspects of their personality. Three days after the essay was sent out he called me, shaken. 'I'm calling because I am really in a bad way and I don't know what to do about it. Perhaps what you are saying in that article applied to me and my situation. Maybe I did her an injustice.'

Love conquers all

Jack loved his fiancée dearly, and keeps a picture of her near his bed to this very day (he is not engaged again or married). Yet their love for each other was not enough to conquer her reluctance to perform the simplest chores and save their beautiful relationship, nor to make him understand that she was different from him. So what is meant when we speak about the power of love?

My answer in situations where practical differences begin to undermine a relationship, is to uphold the romantic ideal. Love can conquer all, or almost all. But the couple in question have to make sure that they do indeed love each other, and not just think they love each other. Conventional wisdom dictates that love is something you feel rather than something you do. But this is wrong. When the Bible says, 'Love your fellow man as yourself,' the Rabbis immediately interpret this to mean, 'Treat him the way you yourself want to be treated.' Love is not measured by the beating of a heart, but by the actions of the hands. The best way, therefore, to gauge the authenticity of the affections of lovers is to see what they *do* about their love.

This point is well made in *Fiddler on the Roof*, the story of Tevya, a poor Jewish milkman, and three of his daughters. All three find love outside the Jewish tradition in that age, culminating in the ultimate form of sacrilege for the father when his youngest daughter marries a Gentile. The subtle message of this simple tale, however, is often overlooked. For this story exemplifies the definition of Jewish love and the way that Judaism has always taught us to distinguish between real and false emotions. When Tevya watches the way each of his three daughters falls in love, they are all starry-eyed, singing, dancing, and immensely happy. In short, they look like they are in love. Infatuation has overtaken them. The young lovers sit on park benches, passionately kissing each other for hours. If that isn't love, what is?

Noticing the lack of such activity in his own marriage, Tevya is confused. His daughter's love life is radically different from his own, and he wonders whether or not he is truly in love with his wife. He runs home and asks his wife Golda, 'Do you love me?' She ignores him. So Tevya asks her again, 'Golda, do you love me?' Golda thinks the question absurd and refuses to answer. But he presses her until finally she exclaims: 'For twenty-five years I've washed your clothes, ironed your shirts, raised your children, cooked your dinners, tended to you when you were sick, and shared this pitiable existence with you without complaint. If that isn't love, what is?'

Besides funny, Golda's point is immensely profound. When we witness a young couple embracing in an airport, kissing passionately, we think that's love. Yet, when another couple, who have been married for many years, meet in the airport and there is no overt display of emotion, we think of the staleness of their marriage. But, though his wife may not fling herself upon her husband as he arrived home, she was waiting there. She took care of their children while he was away, helped run the family business, helped him pack and unpack his bags before he left, and generally served as his partner in all things. A young couple who only *think* they love each other are making out on the living room couch one moment, but are breaking up the next. Yet a married couple love each other enough to work out their differences.

Knowing that you are in love with someone should express itself in the smallest tangible actions. You not only write poetry to one another, but you also take out the garbage so your spouse doesn't have to do it. And perhaps taking out the garbage and saving them the burden is an even greater statement of love than poetry. Because it tacitly says 'I love you so much that I am even willing to do those things that I don't enjoy.' Because I love you,

I don't see these unpleasant things as a terrible burden. When I see you happy, it makes it worthwhile.

True love

A young woman once countered that what I call love in marriage expresses itself only in economic factors and the most practical measures of life, and reflects no higher commitment of the emotions. 'So what kind of love is that?' she said, 'I could make a case that love is much stronger when it does not need that kind of mutual financial gain, or the framework of an institution, in order to remain constant or even flourish.'

But, consider how the rich countries of the world are filled with hypocritical people. These are the people who complain about children who are starving in Somalia, and speak of the plight of youth in the inner city, speaking as though they are emotionally tortured by these tragedies. But then refuse to do a thing about it. When they are approached by charities, they give only an infinitesimal fraction of their wealth.

True love is defined simply as an ability to put someone else before oneself, *in every respect*. Love is selflessness and selflessness is love. Whereas the natural human tendency is to always to seek to be number one, to care for oneself more deeply and more consistently than anything else on earth, true love enables us to reverse this inclination, and reorient it to those things that we love before ourselves. One of the severe drawbacks of mere infatuation is that, like every emotion, it is ephemeral and quickly dissipates.

What if the problem turns out to be insurmountable?

Rebecca and Sam had been married for nine years and had three children. Sam loved his wife very much but could not live with her financial irresponsibility. She spent money constantly, and with no regard to whether or not her husband could keep up with the bills. The things she bought were extravagant and unnecessary. Every day creditors came to the house asking Sam for payment for outstanding invoices. He, knowing nothing of the debt she had accumulated, faced humiliation wherever he went within his local community. He took a second job, but this just caused her to spend even more money. For many years he gave the marriage a chance amidst his wife's promises that she would change. Exasperated, when this did not seem to happen, he offered to pay for a therapist for her to speak with to cure her problem, but she refused to go.

And one day he threw in the towel. 'I simply can't live like this,' he told his wife. Amidst her protestations of how much she loved him and how they should make it work, he left the marital home with the three kids and filed for divorce. I reluctantly supported his decision and Rebecca was shattered and very angry with me. 'It's not my fault, Shmuley, I have a problem, and I admit it. I spend much more than we can afford. But that doesn't mean I don't care about my family.' However, having a problem was no excuse, I told her. Sometimes, loving someone means caring enough to go and seek help for your problems.

The truly selfish person will always find difficulties in relationships. The very definition of being in a relationship is leaving room for another person to enter your life. While there are, indeed, those people who may be prepared to enter as second-class citizens, they are few, and will sooner or later tire of their secondary existence. One must, of course, be absolutely sure that the practical item distancing you from your spouse is so central to your existence that you are willing to break your marriage over it, and we must do everything we can to keep our marriages together. But there is an end to putting the other first. An abusive or totally neglectful spouse who doesn't make an effort to change their behaviour must sometimes, after exerting every effort to try and change their behaviour, be shown the door.

An inability to accommodate your lover's bidding does not necessarily indicate that you do not love them. But it does indicate that you love yourself more. Worryingly enough, the 'me' generation of today's society suffers from a suffocating selfishness that threatens to asphyxiate our hearts and souls. Love is a natural outward effusion, through which we actually derive pleasure from the joy which the party we love experiences. Marriage can just give us that helping hand, because we are forced to work out our difficulties. But, only if we remember to love with a divine love that transcends our tendency towards putting ourselves first.

7. Why should we marry at all?

There is no heaven but women, nor no hell save marriage.
> Thomas Webbe (1660s)

Men marry because they are tired; women, because they are curious; both are disappointed.
> Oscar Wilde. Lord Henry, in *The Picture of Dorian Gray*

I think people really marry far too much; it is such a lottery after all, and for a poor woman a very doubtful happiness.
> Queen Victoria in a letter to her daughter, 1858

It seems obvious to me that few today fully understand the reasons why we marry. Most people say that their reason is love, but it can surely be argued that the need to formalise or consolidate one's love for another human being in the form of an established institution like marriage indicates a deficiency or insecurity in that love. If you truly love each other, then the feelings you have right at this moment should be sufficient to maintain both of you together for the rest of your lives, without the formality of a public ceremony or the need for a verbalised commitment.

And if you don't love each other sufficiently, it is foolish to think that marriage will hold you together. No one wants to remain in a loveless or stultifying marriage. If love is the reason we marry, then marriage is a statement of the potential failure of emotional ties, that emotional attraction is simply insufficient to keep two people together. You should not need words, pieces of paper, or the public serving as witnesses to the act of solidifying your commitment to one another if you harbour a very deep attraction to your beloved.

When one makes a loan to a friend or business acquaintance, it is perfectly acceptable to ask for a promissory note or a valuable to serve as collateral. But if one made the same loan to one's brother or sister, they would be highly offended if collateral were demanded. If you trust someone, then there is no need for the transaction to be guaranteed within an institutionalised framework. One's word, or a statement of commitment on their part, is sufficient. It is only when one does not trust the other sufficiently that contracts become necessary. Similarly, if a man really feels for a woman and vice versa, then they should rightfully feel offended if the person to whom they have pledged their love and commitment demands a formal undertaking to formalise the bond.

Maimonides's view

The great medieval Jewish thinker Maimonides argued in his philosophical masterpiece *Guide to the Perplexed* that the reason the Almighty instituted that humans must marry, and especially in public, was to minimise the friction that would result from inter-human competition for flesh. Many men might compete for the affections and attention of a single woman, thus creating a vast night-club scene, a cattle market where the forces which governed human relationships would be indistinguishable from commercial, market forces. We all know how fierce the competition for material objects is, and how it can sow serious discord among humans. Therefore, in order for humankind to live in peace, an institution which clearly marked people as attached and 'out of competition,' was needed.

I do not intend to dismiss the Maimonidean explanation for marriage. Indeed, anyone knowledgeable of the single's dating scene will know just how profound his explanation is. Today's single scene is fraught with ethical questions created specifically because of relationships that take place outside of marriage. Over the past seven years I have been asked many times by young men whether it is ethical to pursue a friend's girlfriend whom they think has taken a liking to them. After all, they argue, she's not his wife, and the relationship cannot therefore be very serious. One student phrased it in the language of the hunter: 'So long as they're not married, she's still fair game.'

Feeling complete

We little realise that the question of 'Why should we marry at all' is predicated on a flawed perception of humanity. In today's world, we look upon ourselves as being whole, complete individuals. Although we readily acknowledge our blemishes and imperfections, we do not see ourselves as being fundamentally incomplete or deficient. We believe ourselves basically to be good people; perhaps not perfect, but nonetheless not missing anything vital. That cosiness and sense of completion is further enhanced by a good education and a well-paid job which leads to a general sense of security.

But, this assumption of wholesomeness implies that there can be no intrinsic reason for marrying at all. If we are not missing anything in life, why search for a life-long partner? And even if we marry, this philosophy will lead us to discard our spouse the moment things heat up, since we are intrinsically complete even without them.

By way of analogy, if a salesman of third arms approaches a man with two arms and tells him that he has just invented a third arm, and would like to sell him one, the customer will be weary and suspicious. 'I already have two arms. Why do I need a third?' The salesman makes his pitch. 'Just think of it: you could dial the phone, eat a sandwich, and drink your coffee all at the same time. You could carry more groceries into the car from the shop. You could walk the dog, smack your child, and brush your hair all at once. The possibilities are endless!' The customer is convinced and agrees to give it a try.

The first month everything goes well. The third arm really is a tremendous convenience, and it immeasurably enhances his life. But after a few weeks, it begins to play up. One morning it won't wake up at all, complaining it's too tired. The next morning it's temperamental, cantankerously needling its owner that it's not appreciated enough. The third morning it even has the audacity to slap the customer's face, saying that he was being mean and uncaring. 'That's it,' says the customer. 'I've had enough.' And he returns the arm back to the salesman.

But now imagine a man who, God forbid, being physically disabled, was born without a second arm. Along comes a doctor, who says 'We have been experimenting with a second-arm replacement, and would like to provide you with one. I can't guarantee that it will always be useful, obey your commands, or even always work properly.' Still, the patient decides to accept the arm, and although he experiences the same problems that the man with the third arm did, he sticks with it, feeling grateful that he has the second arm at all. He perseveres with the arm because he acknowledges his state of incompletion. But in the case of the man with two arms, the third arm is superfluous; an added extra. If it works, it works. If it doesn't, you get rid of it. To the man with only one arm, the second mechanical arm is an intrinsic blessing, even if it is not perfect. To the man with two arms, the third arm is only a blessing if it brings him happiness. Otherwise, it is an easily discarded nuisance.

Man and woman are one

This is the radical difference between modern opinion and Judaism. The Bible does not play along with this notion that we are perfect. Instead it sees a man or woman as only one half of a potentially whole being. Each person is simply incomplete by him or herself. No job, acquisition of knowledge, or praise from other human beings can ever change this. It is an anatomical *and* spiritual fact, which is rooted in the very constitution of man.

Most people would interpret the Biblical story of creation as saying that Adam was male, and that he searched for a female who was later given to him when God caused him to sleep and removed one of his ribs, thereafter covering it with flesh and creating womankind. Such an interpretation, however, places a wholly negative light on female qualities by implying that they are not in some way intrinsic to a human being. It implies that God created women as an afterthought, and this is rightly resented by many women.

But, the ancient Jewish interpretation of the Bible has always maintained that God created Adam in the Garden of Eden as a hybrid of both male and female. The traditional Jewish interpretation of these verses in Genesis suggests that the word 'tzela,' usually translated as 'rib,' here means 'side.' Adam was not the first man, but rather the first *human*, and he was an androgynous being, possessing both masculine and feminine dimensions. When Adam fell asleep, God removed an entire side, the feminine side, from His creature, and the result was the splitting of the first human being into Adam, who remained male, and Eve, who became female.

The result was that each side was no longer complete and now depended on rejoining and reuniting with their lost half in order to achieve wholeness. This idea that man and woman are two halves of an original hermaphrodite creature, is also implicit in the word 'sex' itself. It derives from the Latin word 'secare,' which means to cut or divide into sections. Rather than just living together, marriage brings about the reunification of a once-complete organism that was separated at creation's outset. Therefore, marriage is perforce a religious institution. It is only He, who separated us at the beginning of time, who can once again fuse us together as one under the wedding canopy. Indeed, the ancient Jewish mystics maintained that husband and wife shared a single soul that was also rejoined when they married.

What about people who remain single

I recognise that what I am writing can be viewed quite negatively by those who are still single. Is someone who has not married, or who will never marry, incomplete? There can be no doubt that a single person can lead a very wholesome, satisfying, and complete life, accomplish great things, and make significant contributions that can enhance the lot of all humanity. The Talmud tells of Rabbi Yonasan ben Uziel, the greatest disciple of Hillel the Elder, who was one of the leading and most respected Sages of Israel. So engrossed was he in the study of Torah that he never married. His mastery of Jewish law, and indeed his contributions to the development and codification of Jewish thought are almost without parallel. Nevertheless, he was roundly criticised by the Talmud itself in spite of his apparent mastery.

This does not trivialise the important contribution that he made to Jewish life. What it does mean is that he would have been far more complete had he married. As the Bible states, 'It is not good for man to be alone.' I am friendly with many singles and confirmed bachelors and spinsters. Yet few of them remain so as a matter of conviction. Rather, they remain single because, for a variety of reasons, they either did not find a partner suitable enough to their tastes to marry, or were burned in a previous relationship and fear being hurt again. Man is a universe to himself, but there are different levels in human completion for all of us. While the single person who endeavours his or her best to lead a loving and decent life and contribute to their environment and community is complete on one level, they still lacks a greater form of completion that can only be found through finding one's other half and getting married.

The same is true of friendship and all other human relationships. We can lead life on our own, but the more people we have to share the warmth and light of human experience, the more enriched our life will be. In the Bible, man's soul is made analogous to a candle; when two flames are put near each other, they naturally incline toward one another. All of us are looking to share our light with someone we love, and the highest form is marriage, a union in which we join together becoming one flesh.

8. Marriage, a relationship based on fragility.

Why does a woman work ten years to change a man's habits and then complain that he's not the man she married?

Barbra Streisand.

A good marriage lasts forever. A bad one just seems to.

Anonymous

One of the most difficult emotions experienced by students when they first arrive in Oxford is loneliness. For many it is the fact that they are leaving home, often for the first time. For others, loneliness and a sense of isolation is induced because of the large workload greeting students upon their arrival. Yet others feel a sense of solitude and isolation because of Oxford's greater emphasis on intellectual achievement than emotional bonding. Oxford has one of the highest suicide rates of any University in the world. As I write these lines, just last week a student killed himself after breaking up with his girlfriend. He asked her to come outside so that he could tell her something, and as she emerged he hurled himself under an approaching rubbish-truck.

What is loneliness?

But, for all of us the awesome power of loneliness is indivisibly a part of our existence. At the beginning of the book of Genesis, the Bible discusses the loneliness of the first man, Adam. Every animal had a helpmate, a companion, but Adam did not. God, in His kindness, created for him a partner whom Adam called Eve.

But why did Adam feel lonely in the first place? After all, he was living in the Garden of Eden and had all the angels with whom he could talk and hang out.

Adam's loneliness, according to the Rabbis, was caused by the fact that the angels were perfect and did not need anything from Adam. The angels being whole and complete could receive no contribution of substance from him. They didn't come to Adam with their problems because they had none. They didn't ask him his advice because they their lives weren't in a mess. And they certainly didn't need to be comforted with a hug. In short, he needed them, but they did not need him. He was lonely because he could not give.

With the creation of Eve, Adam now had someone who, like him, was imperfect, and thus needed his love as much as he needed hers. He had someone whose life he could touch; a being whose heart was made of flesh and not of perfection. Someone who made him feel that his existence actually made a difference to her, a being who needed to be held and kept warm. This made Adam feel necessary and cured the pangs of loneliness.

Being needed makes us feel content

Therefore, we do not feel lonely because we have no one with whom to share our lives. Rather, loneliness overtakes us when we feel that we are not necessary, when those who do share our lives do not appreciate our contribution. Loneliness hits us particularly when we suddenly discover, as the student above, that we are not needed. This explains why individuals who have discovered that their spouse has had an affair describe it as the most severe pain they have ever experienced, as bad, God forbid, as a bereavement. 'After everything I did for him, all the years of working to put him through College, washing his shirts, making him dinner, this is what he did to me!' Nothing hurts as much as being made to feel replaced and discarded.

But I have also met many women who are married and still profess themselves to be the loneliest people on earth. When you are married to a man who is a workaholic and who is successful enough that he has the public's approbation, he often shows his wife little attention because he corroborates his value with factors outside the marriage. He doesn't have to come home on time, and he doesn't have to consult her on the most important questions of his life. He has lawyers and business partners for that. Not surprisingly, the primary reason, according to every survey, for a wife's infidelity is neglect on the part of her husband. Over 80 per cent of men who cheat on their wives, still claim to love their wives. But only six percent of women who love their husbands will cheat on them.

Acknowledging that you are insecure

Ever since Karl Marx declared religion to be the opiate of the masses, religious people have been fighting a rearguard action, attempting to show how they embrace religion for the right reasons and not because of their insecurity. I, however, have no compunction in admitting that I need God and rely upon Him as the rock of my salvation, that I acknowledge that without God's providence and blessing, every effort is for nought, and that from the constraints and vulnerability and loneliness of human life I call out to my Creator for his love and protection. The highest form of love is to need someone, and those who cannot acknowledge a deeply felt need unfortunately cannot love. Those who cannot acknowledge their vulnerability – who are afraid to rely on someone else – cannot truly become one with their partner. True love entails a feeling of helplessness when we are not in the company of our beloved.

Similarly, sharing a relationship with someone who is in touch with his or her insecurities is the only relief from loneliness. Loneliness comes about not when there is no-one around whom you need, but rather when there is no-one around who needs you. The misery of having no-one around who requires your love is far greater than having no-one to give you love. If there were no human insecurities, people would still relate with another. But they would never become enmeshed and intertwined with each other. Sharing a relationship with a profoundly secure person (if there is such a thing) can be the loneliest experience of all because, while they cherish you they don't depend on you.

Dropping your guard

There is no more complete or sublime method by which to express this devotion to others, or to receive love from others, than through marriage, an institution which compels a human being to put another person before them, always. Being a parent makes us feel needed at all times, and thus makes one feel more whole and able to rise above loneliness. Being a spouse, and needing our partner, allows them to love us. This is the ingenious solution provided by the Creator to ensure that, if we accept them, our anxieties about our imperfections are always assuaged, leading to life-affirming, rather than destructive results.

Think what a difference it makes when we are needed. My wife and I called around to see our friend Tanya shortly after the birth of her first child. She looked radiantly happy with her new-born son. 'Do you know when I felt the most special being a mother?' she said. 'It was when I took the baby to Tesco's and put him down to look for the Nappies section. It struck me that he just stayed there. Had I left him there he'd still be there now. He needs me even for his mobility. It feel wonderful to be so important to somebody!'

Healthy insecurity

Far from distancing ourselves from a relationship built around assuaging our loneliness or insecurity, we should thank God that in our spouse we have someone who loves us and needs us always. In Judaism, when we toast our fellow human beings over wine or an alcoholic beverage, we say, 'L'Chaim', which means not 'To Life', as many suppose, but rather 'To Lives,' in the plural. No-one could live life by themselves. We all need someone else. So there's no point in toasting life, because life that is not shared is unliveable. Life only has meaning when it is shared with others, and we are strengthening and enriching their existence as well.

Manis Friedman tells the story of a woman who complained to him that she was not happily married and was contemplating a divorce. Amazingly, she conceded that her husband was always warm, affectionate, sensitive, and caring. 'So what's the problem he asked?' She answered that she wasn't sure if in his heart-of-hearts he really and truly loved her. 'Lady,' Rabbi Friedman answered. 'You don't need a divorce. You need a spanking.'

The difference between healthy and unhealthy insecurity resides in the focus on action. If a husband or wife is treated marvellously by their spouse, yet they still feel insecure and look for imperfections and supposed slights in the relationship, then their insecurities might be said to have got the better of them. Get a grip.

But if someone is being treated badly, or if a wife is utterly neglected by her husband – even if he or she professes love to their spouse – they can hardly be accused of merely being insecure. God made us incomplete, which means that vulnerability and loneliness come to us naturally. What we must always assure, therefore, is that these insecurities cause us to be more sensitive to the people around us. Our natural insecurities can either undermine our lives by making us arrogant, paranoid and tyrannical, or very uncertain or weak, all ensuring that people stay away. But, our insecurities can also teach us caring and empathy whereby we come to understand the vulnerability of all humankind and everyone's needs to feel love and appreciation.

To be sure, we cannot allow the comfort of a relationship to overwhelm us to the point that we smother our partner with love and never allow them outside our sight. Relationships built on extreme insecurity are sure to fail. But within a healthy medium, we have every right to revel in the companionship which marriage provides. Once we have acquired this, we must not allow insecurity to consume us, especially through searching the inner recesses of our partner's heart to see if they really love us. Focus rather on action. A husband or wife who make the effort to do the right thing in marriage and keep their spouses constantly happy, are very precious indeed.

9. Why parental love ceases to be sufficient

And Isaac brought [Rebecca] into the tent of Sarah his mother, and
he took her and she became his wife, and he loved her. And Isaac
was finally comforted after the loss of his mother.

Genesis 24: verse 67

Mummy, you know the vase you were always worried I would
break? Well, your worries are over.   Anonymous

Several times a week parents of a Jewish twenty or thirty-some-
thing will call me and pour out their sorrow over a child who is
either seriously dating, or engaged to a non-Jew. As the Jewish
community's numbers are seriously dwindling, the subject of
intermarriage is most painful. 'You call yourself a Rabbi? You
should be ashamed of yourself. My son was raised in an orthodox
home. I gave him life, warm clothes, a good education, and love.
He knows better than to marry a non-Jew. My wife and I wish we
were in our grave. But you have welcomed him at your table and
treat him as if he's done nothing wrong. We haven't spoken to him
in three years. Now a Rabbi betrays us. Disgraceful.' They may
say this even if they realise that the Rabbi has a duty to ensure
that such couples retain a strong affiliation with the Jewish
community.

Parental love vs. romantic love

Our parents love us to bits. And sometimes their love is so intense
that it is even expressed as censure for something we've done
which they maintain is very bad for us. But as we mature we find
that the solace and comfort which their love once provided dimin-
ishes and becomes less important to us. Suddenly all we can think
of is the other sex. We want to find the man or woman of our
dreams. But for parents this is a difficult moment (as in the story
above) for they argue that compared to our parents the man or
woman we are after is a complete stranger. Yet, we find their
affection intensely more satisfying than that of our parents. Why?
Romantic love seems to be a very poor route to achieve fulfil-

ment anyway. Whereas our parents seem to find merit in virtually everything we say, our verbal pronouncements to our romantic partners will either make a favourable or unfavourable impression. Our actions either keep our partners and friends firmly attached to us, or running in the opposite direction. Our parents will never divorce us, but our spouses might. Why give it all up?

The answer is that although our parents love us dearly, they have no choice but to do so. Their genes make them love us. In the same way that a drop of rain emitted by a cloud must fall to the earth, so too our parents must fall in love with us. Our parents have made no conscious choice to do so. It is in their nature. In many ways it is as if a gun is being held to their head and they are told that they must cherish and adore their children.

The beauty and strength of this also demonstrates its weakness. When a teenage girl hears her mother tell her that she is the prettiest in the neighbourhood, is her mother telling her the truth? When a father tells his son that he is so intelligent and mature, does this make it so? A mother tells her son that he is handsome, intelligent, and charming. She loves him with all her heart, and of course she is going to say, and think that. Parents are able to give us everything, except the knowledge that we are unique people who can earn such love through our own devices.

What we really, really want

What we must remember is that the greatest human aspiration is not to be loved, but to be *special*, to be distinguishable from all others on our planet. This is one of the things, for example, which bothers people most when approached by demographic pollsters. They don't just want to be another statistic. They want to be individuals, who are different from their neighbours and relatives, who are special, singular, and unique. We feel this to be so very strongly.

In the depths of our very heart we know that we are irreplaceable. In the same way that no two people look alike, no two people actually are alike. Every soldier wants to be promoted, every artist wants to be recognised, and every human being wants to be chosen. There is a unique contribution to the world that only we can make.

In fact our early lives can be wrecked by an absence of feeling unique. We feel torn asunder as children when we feel neglected by our parents. 'Am I not special?' we ask ourselves. 'Who will make me feel that way?' And we may spend the rest of our life in self-doubt and insecurity. Similarly, every one of us fears that if we don't wake up tomorrow morning, perhaps, nobody would even notice, nobody would even care. We fear being alive and yet remaining unremarkable.

The power of romantic love

When we are teenagers we are consumed by a similar fear of nothingness. We start to wonder about the attention of our parents. How often do we hear of young people taking their own lives and leaving messages behind that say in essence, 'Now you'll notice me. When I was alive you ignored me. You may not have noticed my presence then, but you will certainly notice my absence when I am dead.'

But, our partners make us feel special precisely because, unlike our parents, they choose us. When they tell us we are beautiful, we believe them, because nothing compelled them to say it. Moreover, they could have made the same declaration of love to countless other people. Our lover has recognised our unique beauty in comparison to and over and above all others. And this recognition comes specifically through the process of choice. Our own state of specialness is confirmed by the simple fact that our lover could have chosen anyone to profess their love to. There was nothing compelling them to dedicate themselves to us specifically. So it must be that indeed we are special.

Marriage and the divine

Marriage provides us with that ultimate, divine mirror which allows us to see ourselves for what we are. The Bible declares that each of us is created in the image of God. This means that in the same way that God is the one and only, so too each of us is the one and only. Because we are all created in the image of God we posses a fragment of the divine within us which we can realise. But, it comes at a price. We shall never find full satisfaction or happiness in life until we have realised how important our partners are for that aspect of ourselves. We must constantly make an effort to remain in touch with our divine essence.

Marriage, then, becomes more than something which solidifies human affection. Rather, it is a psychological necessity. Because being chosen by a stranger in a non-coercive way for a life-long commitment is the ultimate corroboration of our uniqueness. Therefore, when problems arise in our marriage, rather than just immediately search for the escape hatch, we should remember the strong completion of our intrinsic selves which marriage brings, and always seek to work the problems out.

Part Four

Marriage and Divorce

1. Is divorce ever a good thing?

A man never knows the value of a woman's love until he pays
maintenance. Anonymous

One major reason for divorce is that husbands who promised they
would die for their wives, failed to deliver. Anonymous

He owed his success to his first wife and his second wife to his
success. Anonymous

The heaviest object in the world is the body of the woman you have
ceased to love. Marquis de Luc de Clapiers Vauenargues

I have a policy of never giving up a free meal (or anything else
free for that matter). So when Maureen called up exhilarated and
excited, 'Quick, get Debbie, I'm taking you all out to dinner', I was
delighted. But when she explained 'I'm officially divorced. I'm rid
of that bastard forever.' I felt the need to violate my principals,
'Look Maureen, we'll of course come out to dinner with you, but
not as a celebration for your divorce. Let's celebrate your being
happy, without being specific.' My friend got very offended. 'You
know how unhappy I was with him and how much he used me.
And now he's gone, and if you're not happy for me, then it's just
your tough luck.' 'Maureen,' I said, 'if God forbid someone needed
chemotherapy to rid themselves of disease, we wouldn't be party-
ing for that, because it's a necessary but not a good thing.'

My spouse, my child

Suppose you can't have children, and would like to adopt. But
before making the decision to adopt, you tell the adoption board
that you're very happy to take a child home, but only on the

condition that if things do not work out you have the right to return him or her to the agency. Would you condone that attitude? The answer is, 'Of course not.' By making this condition they are not treating the baby as their child, but rather as some sort of boarder. Their commitment to the child remains tenuous and ephemeral, completely unlike the intrinsic bond which exists between parent and child.

This is exactly the point of marriage too. When you fail to commit yourself before a given relationship, this is a statement of the relationship being transitory. Parents who refuses to commit themselves to their child are saying 'This will be my charge, but not my child'. And the same applies to those who only live together as opposed to marrying. Marrying actually helps us fall more deeply in love with each other, because when a woman hears that a man is prepared to commit himself to her for the rest of his life, she cannot help but feel swept off her feet by this vow to remain unconditionally devoted to her.

Understanding what divorce means

Divorce is essentially a separation of oneself from oneself. Once we view our married partners as those who complete us, and thus are an actual and vital part of ourselves, we understand that divorce becomes a justified recourse only in the most acute circumstances. To see one's spouse as a part of oneself, as a limb, as it were, exposes what divorce is about. Although I am readily prepared to dispose of a car which causes more anguish than pleasure, the same is not true of my arm. One is fully prepared to stay the course in order to fix problems with a limb, however serious, since to severe one's own arm is to mutilate oneself, and to lose an arm or a leg is to be incomplete.

In this respect, I treat divorce like the decision not to resuscitate a dying patient because their quality of life has deteriorated too far amidst incessant pain. In these circumstances, a relative would hardly say, 'Boy, thank goodness he's dead. I mean, when he was alive all he did was feel pain. Dying was simply the best thing that could have happened to him!' A man or a woman who are getting divorced are not lucky. At most, they've done what they had to do. But it shall always remain a tragedy. It represents man at his weakest. It is a statement of man's perfunctory and transitory nature.

Divorce, an act of necessity

This is not to say that divorce is never necessary. Studs Terkel called his celebrated book on World War II, *The Good War*, because in it he described how everyone agreed on the justice of the war and how it had to be fought. This in stark contrast to World War I which comprised just meaningless and wholesale slaughter of innocent combatants. The Nazi evil which stalked Europe simply had to be defeated and in this respect it was 'good war.' I think, however, that his title misses the point. He would have been far more accurate had he called his book 'The *Necessary* War.' War is never good. It is either necessary or unnecessary. It would have been good if Hitler had never been born. But once he was and assumed power, it became necessary to defeat him.

Likewise, because God is compassionate, He does not force a man and a woman who loathe each other to live together. To do so would be unspeakably cruel. People have a right to find happiness in life, and if after exerting every effort to make a marriage work, its participants still feel miserable, they must dissolve their union. Nonetheless, the Talmud says that God's holy altar weeps for every couple who divorce. It is only a necessary outlet for two people who cannot live together in harmony and love.

My own experience as a child

Being a product of a broken home, it still bothers me till this very day that there are children of similar homes who will actually speak about their parent's divorce as if it were a good thing. They say 'Thank heavens my parents finally got divorced! They were just killing each other. They're both better off this way.' Surely they are mistaken. Our parents would have been better off being happily married.

My whole life was affected by my parents' divorce. It heightened my insecurities and left me feeling that nothing in life really works. To me the world was made of a bunch of broken pieces, incongruent parts that can come together for a time, but ultimately never fit. How else is a child to feel when the archetypal relationship, which brought him or her into this world, dissolves amidst great acrimony? If so, where would I eventually fit in? I looked forward neither to happiness, nor to peace. When a doctor recently asked me in Synagogue if I thought that his recent divorce from his wife of sixteen years would have any affect on their son, I said, 'It's like asking whether discovering that the sun won't shine tomorrow, or that the body has no immune system, will have any affect on one's outlook on life.'

In life, we're always sure that there is some fail-safe system, some safety net, something that will stop the ultimate calamity from happening. But, once your parents divorce, you're no longer so sure. OK, death also overtakes us. But at least there we concede that there is little that we can do. Life and death are not in our control. But marriage and divorce are. Divorce is a sign that ultimately humans are not in control of their lives and destinies. We got married with the intent of being happy. And yet, it turned out miserable, even though we were in control the entire time. So you end up becoming a cynic who scoffs at hearing of other people's happiness because you don't believe it possible. Not in this world, at least.

The negative cycle of divorce

Once I was speaking with an Oxford student whose parents are divorced. Most of her friends also come from broken homes. She was intensely hostile to marriage and was adamant that living together provided a far better alternative. As far as she was concerned, the only genuine and coherent argument for marriage arises if someone is religious. Therefore, because a person like her does not live by religious tenets, and therefore cannot be classified as living in sin, marriage, she argued, was utterly meaningless. Her group of friends added that the only reason people still marry is to conform with social convention. As all their arguments were negative, I didn't need to be a prophet to guess that every single one of them had divorced parents or parents whose marriage was severely unhappy.

The negative cycle of divorce is the imprint it leaves on second generations. Studies show that children from divorced backgrounds are 50 per cent more likely to divorce themselves. And according to this student and her group of friends, all the people whom they knew and had been married for more than five years were miserable. Marriage was no more than 'trouble and strife,' even with someone with whom they were in love. The world's largest club consists of children of divorce. But, we who form the members of this club have the greatest challenge of all: to break, with the help of God, this terrible cycle of pain and despair which marital strife breeds and to bequeath to our children a world filled with love, light, and hope.

2. Your spouse's impossible flaws

I have three pets at home which answer to the same purpose as a husband; I have a dog which growls every morning, a parrot which swears all afternoon, and a cat that comes home late at night.

Marie Corelli

She wanted a husband and put an advertisement in the Personal Column. She got 200 replies, all saying: 'You can have mine.'

Anonymous

Rabbi Aryeh Levine, a saintly Sage who lived fifty years ago in Jerusalem, described how once he saw a close friend of his very late at night at the hospital. His friend seemed perfectly fit, so Rabbi Levine enquired why he was at the hospital in the middle of the night. The man pointed to his aged wife who was limping behind him and said, 'Reb Aryeh, *our* foot hurts.' Not, 'This darned wife of mine has got this lousy foot that keeps me up in the middle of the night,' but rather, '*We* have a problem so we both came here in middle of the night to sort it out.' 'My wife's problems are my problems since we are one.'

Within marriage we must make a conscious effort not to forget that one's spouse is one's other half, the person we love and care for most. The woman with whom you now argue is not a stranger, she is your wife. And the man whom you are so disappointed with is not some supermarket checkout clerk, he is the father of your children. To harm your spouse is to harm yourself. To fall out with them is to fall out with yourself. If they are unhappy, you are going to be unhappy. That spirit of gloom which will pervade the house will invade your home, for both of you share that home. Your spouse is a part of you, your other half.

An aggressive spouse

I mentioned this to Nancy, who came to talk to me after another terrible fight with her husband. He had a bad temper. He was not violent. But when he lost his cool, he would verbally abuse her, telling her how stupid she was. She could bear it because arguments this serious only took place, at most, on a monthly basis. But the terrible pressures of opening a new business made Gary even more temperamental, and he was blowing up at her several times a week. 'I can't live with this man and his terrible temper' she said. 'I want to be married, but I am miserable. I can't imagine staying with him any longer unless he deals with his problem.'

'I think it would be very helpful,' I replied 'if you didn't speak about *his* problem. Since you are married, his temper is not solely his problem. It is the problem of both of you. And if you saw it in this way, you wouldn't think of abandoning him. It does not excuse his behaviour which has no justification and must change. But the chances of him changing are far greater when both your energies are thrown at it, rather than when he is asked to change on his own. I know a woman whose son was born with a terrible stutter and speech impediment. She is far from rich, and yet twice a week she must take three hours of uncompensated time from work and drive her son one hour in each direction to a speech therapist. Yet, never once did I hear her say 'It is my son's problem.' Her attitude is that she as a mother has a problem.'

Marriage is not just a human decision, or a socio-economic arrangement. It is in Judaism the Almighty Himself who determines who will marry whom. The Talmud declares that God's most difficult task is serving as a matchmaker. He finds it a greater challenge than parting the Red Sea. A husband and wife are two halves of one soul who are separated prior to their descent from heaven to earth. Under the 'chupa', the wedding canopy, they are reunited as one. And they emerge as a one. A man's wife has always been his wife, just as his child has always been his child. Indeed, the feeling that one just 'bumped' into one's spouse in a completely arbitrary way is one of the most destructive of all attitudes in marriage. Anything which we view as having occurred 'arbitrarily' is something to which we will feel far less devoted.

The effect of marriage

A friend of mine was experiencing severe marital difficulties and I went to see him and his wife to explore if I could help iron out their differences. I was astonished to discover that my friend's father was very upset with me. 'Why did you interfere?' he asked me. 'She is wrong for him, and the entire family wants him to get rid of her. In fact, we've already started looking for someone else. We're going to introduce him to someone better.'

'Someone better?' I asked, 'But he's a married man! How can you ask a married man to take someone else out? And what do you mean by wanting to get rid of her? She is not some stranger. For goodness sake, she is his wife!' 'People who marry have been joined as one flesh in he most profound, possible way.'

This merging as one is a most potent feeling. Once on an ordinary Monday afternoon, I returned home for lunch from my office and my wife greeted me with an immense smile and these words: 'You're not going to believe how beautiful this is!' and with this she picked up a handsomely bound red book entitled, *The Wolf Shall Lie With the Lamb*. It was the first copy of my book, which my United States publisher had sent. I had waited two years since the completion of the manuscript to see it in published form and I was ecstatic. But, I focused more on the joy of my wife than my own and something puzzled me: she was just as elated as excited as me, and yet it was I who had written the book!

It was then that the full force of what I described finally hit me. It was not my book, or a book that my wife could celebrate because it had been written by her husband. Rather, it was our book. Anything I had written was equally hers. Any insights offered in that book largely derived from ongoing conversations with my wife on all subjects of life. When she showed people the book she was showing something that was hers. (My wife, however, firmly disclaims any association with this book on sex: as far as she is concerned it was written by the Rabbi Hyde side of my character, and she has been walking around the Jewish religious sections of London with a brown paper bag over her head ever since). This bond, which is there whether we are conscious of it all the time or not, is what we have to keep in mind when we deal with the rough side of our spouse's personality. If your spouse has a problem with being too critical, it is *both* your problem, and you must tackle it as a couple to make it disappear.

3. Adultery, such fun?

With all my heart. Whose wife shall it be?
> John Horne Tooke, replying to the
> suggestion that he take a wife

When a man marries his mistress, she leaves a vacancy.
> James Goldsmith's maîtresse

Those who cheat on their spouses are convinced that their partners in crime believe them to be sexy and amorous. With all the attention and gifts he lavishes on her, the adulterous husband is under the impression that the woman with whom he fools around finds him romantic, caring and sexy. Studies, however, reveal the opposite. Most mistresses of married men believe them to be unimpressive cowards who cheat and vacillate, offending all parties in turn. She may indeed be attracted to him, and she may indeed find him charming, filled with masculine energy. But she also finds him hypocritical, unfaithful, untrustworthy, duplicitous, weak, and an outright liar.

The *Hite Report on Love, Passion, and Emotional Violence* quotes many examples of what women really think of unfaithful husbands with whom they share an affair. One woman comments, 'At about twenty I flirted with a married man who told me how bad his marriage/wife was. Something might have happened but I met his wife – she was a beautiful, nice mother of four with a jerk for a husband.' Another woman writes: 'I was infatuated with a married man for a short while during my first year in college. I came to see him as a real wimp for limping along in his relationship with his wife and decided to save myself all this bother and hassle by breaking off with him. We never did sleep together a second time. He was a nice guy, and an extraordinary artist, but he just didn't have enough character.'

Indeed, no matter how sexy or alluring a man's mistress finds him, there will never be security in the relationship. Even if he runs off with her and marries her, pledging himself to her eternally, she cannot shake what she knows to be the truth: that he is the kind of man who gets easily bored with one woman. That rather than admit his faults, he blames everything on his wife. That after they marry and he comes home late one night, no matter how much he promises her that he was simply working late, she will always have to worry that perhaps he is cheating on her as well.

Nomadic passion

In the book of Genesis, Esau, elder brother of Jacob, sells his birthright to his younger brother for a plate of porridge, thereby squandering his privileges as a firstborn. Why did he do it? Well, he felt hungry. The Rabbis explain that he had had an extremely busy day. Among other things, he had murdered a man, and stolen his wife. This brief mention of Esau's adultery is not incidental but central to the plot.

What the Bible tells us is that the adulterer is like Esau, a nomad, a hunter, a man who lives from day to day. A man with no permanence and whose existence is entirely fly-by-night. He eats the beast of the field and makes his bed wherever it is most convenient. Today he personifies all-too-many modern day men and women who think that life is only about excitement and instant thrills, who pursue nought but that which is instantly gratifying to the senses, who have no appreciation or pleasure from anything deep and lasting.

Like Esau, the adulterer convinces himself that he is an explorer, though he really is a wanderer. He thinks to himself he is not a bad person, but merely broadening his sexual experience and taste. He does not intend to harm his marriage. He will argue that he loves his wife, and what is so wrong with just a bit of excitement and pleasure? But, like Esau he has gone from being a man of strength and commitment, to being a weakling who whose life vacillates and is tempest-tossed by every passing wind. He will always be on the move, for he has lost the anchor of his personality.

This lifestyle may indeed lead to passion, in the same way that the man of the jungle's life might be construed to be more exciting than the grocery-store salesman. But it is a false excitement born of disorientation. Like the man who shoots a drug into his arm whenever life becomes too unbearable or monotonous, so too, the adulterer leaves the security of the home and prowls out into the night whenever he feels that his life needs some adventure. What he refuses to see, however, is the transitory nature of that excitement and the way in which he scars himself. Like Esau he will remain a nomad, never achieving the wholesomeness that is the lot of Jacob, who finds his sense of completion through disciplined relationships, commitment, and a life of public and private duty, none of which preclude the possibility and necessity for marital passion and romance.

The spirit of madness

The Talmud declares that no one sins unless gripped by a spirit of madness. This statement, one of my favourite Talmudic quotes, simply states the obvious: that if the average person were to think through all the consequences of their transgression, they would never do it. We sin because we just don't think. Like all sins, the delights of adultery don't really exist. Sure, for a few moments or even weeks the pleasure is there. But compared to the infinite misery which this is all leading to, there will be scarce memories of pleasure. Once your life begins to self-destruct and your spouse abandons you, you will wish that you kept your pants on.

Let's say you go ahead with the affair. You continue seeing your lover and develop real passion and excitement. You will then arrive at the point where you will have to make a choice between your spouse and your lover. And don't fool yourself into thinking the two can coexist. For, they cannot. Every act of love with your illicit lover is a stab in the heart of your other half.

Whatever energy you are putting into your affair is being depleted from you marriage. The real sin of adultery is not so much a sin of *commission* – doing something wrong – but rather, it is a sin of *omission* – failing to do something right. There is no marriage on the planet which can survive the complete redirection of love and sexual focus which is involved in having an adulterous partner. And whatever interest you are showing your lover, you are not showing to your spouse. When the reason for this is found out, spouses will bring the rafters in the ceiling down rather than allow their humiliation to continue. In every act of adultery a man and woman hurt themselves; because to hurt one's spouse is, literally, to hurt oneself.

Marriage is a hungry animal that needs to be fed and replenished constantly, and adultery is like someone who takes water pipes leading into his home and diverts them to his neighbour's home. No one in his house will survive. His marriage will be like an arid desert, bereft of life-nourishing sensitivity and affection. No one can retain their marital passion towards their spouse when they are expending it in such vast quantities on someone else. Ironically, this is more true for women than it is for men, as psychologist Carol Botwin explains: 'Most men, even when they have some affection for the other woman, are able to keep an affair from taking over their emotional lives. This is in direct contrast to women, who tend to become consumed. In letter after letter, case history after case history, wives confessed that their heads were totally occupied by their lovers.'

But for any cuckolded spouse it is true that the anger and pain of betrayal will find expression specifically in their married life. In the Bible it is written that God made Eve as a 'helpmate for Adam.' But the Hebrew word 'for' also translates as 'against.' The Talmud explains that when a man loves his wife, she becomes 'for' him, a helpmate. When he neglects or abuses, her, she becomes 'against' him. While he has found new life, she experiences a pain equivalent to death. Her former marriage goodwill oozes out slowly, and she finds every reason in the world to quarrel with you. Her friends see her and will hate you for snuffing out the fire in her soul.

And ultimately no real benefit lies in store for the adulterer. A dentist I knew had an affair. The woman insisted that he leave his wife for her or she too would leave. 'It's a difficult choice,' he told me. 'I'm crazy about this new woman, but I love my children, and I guess I also love my wife.' I told him, 'Once the mistress is always available, she loses her mystique and the sex its forbidden excitement. You will give up your wife and get nothing in return. Since you haven't learned how to bring newness and novelty into an existing relationship, you will be just as bored of your new wife the moment you start living with her, and the cycle will just repeat itself. Rather than destroying your life and your family, go back to your wife and make an all-out effort to reignite the spark of your marriage.' He disagreed, left his wife and devastated the family for the other woman, and, indeed, eighteen months later he was as bored with the new woman as he was with his wife and ended up leaving her as well.

Statistics show that this is a common occurrence. 80 per cent of all men who leave their wives for another woman end up leaving the new woman within the first year; and no wonder. If a man cannot learn to find vertical renewal in his marriage – unearthing novel and exciting aspects of the relationship – all he is capable of is bed-hopping.

One night stands

But suppose your fling does not develop into an affair. You will still lose out. Once, when the great Rabbi Yochanan ben Zakkai lay dying, his students asked him to bless them before he expired. 'I bless you that you should all learn to fear God as much as you fear your fellow man.' His students were aghast. 'Is that all? You only wish us to fear heaven as much as we fear humans, and no more.' Rabbi Yochanan responded, 'Whenever a man is about to sin, and he sees that people are watching him, he refrains from sinning. It would be wonderful if we feared God watching us just as much.'

Sin causes us to develop a dual personality. If Carol slanders her friend Susan behind her back, then the next time they meet Carol will have to hide her real feelings and actions from Susan. The real loser here is not Susan but Carol. She now has a whole dimension of her personality that must be hidden and imprisoned. In doing so, Carol develops a split personality. She can never just be herself around Susan ever again. She will always have to repress and submerge her real feelings. And the more she gossips about other people behind their backs, the more pervasive her dual identity becomes, until she has no rest in any of her relationships.

The same is true, and much more so, of marriage. Its prime beauty is that there is one person in the world with whom a man or a woman can be totally natural. But now, every time a phone bill arrives at the house, it is a moment of anxiety. 'Did I remember not to call my mistress from the house?' Every credit card bill might give you away. After a while, your own home becomes a hellish den for you, as you are permanently on pins and needles, thinking you will be discovered And you had better remember your lies as well, so that you don't give yourself away. Indeed, you will have to tell bigger and bigger lies in order to cover over the smaller ones.

What is the point of this secret, unshared memory? For example, Do we ever take a break from being a parent to our children? Do we sneak out at night to read a bed time story to our neighbour's child who is good at maths and never gets into trouble? Do we tell them, 'I know you are not my son, but tonight, for once, I would really like to pretend you are and see what its like. But don't tell Mikey. It must remain *our* secret.' Cheating on our children is an absurd prospect because we see our children as our own flesh and blood. And a husband and wife who practise kosher sex to become one flesh, will likewise preclude the possibility of ever cheating on one another.

Adultery, a call of nature

Of course, the adulterous partner will argue that they felt forced into it. They were not looking to hurt anyone, least of all themselves. They merely gave in to lust and desire. But it had little to do with them. They will begin to cite neglect on the part of their spouse as an excuse to justify their indiscretion. And if they are not loved, or if there is no passion in their marriage, what are they do? Don't they deserve some measure of happiness in their lives? And, really when they met their mistress adultery was the last thing on their mind. It kind of happened by default.

But who are they kidding? They do deserve all the passion they want. But, like spineless creatures, they are taking the easy way out. In an age where couples try and get along and allow themselves to fall out of love slowly, they may well have a legitimate complaint that their excitement has been lost within their marriage. But, instead of working hard and regaining the passion in their marriage, they are allowing events to take control of their lives. The solution is instead to make your wife into your mistress, your husband into your secret lover, and make your marriage into an illicit affair.

Being a great person

There exist two kinds of human greatness. The first is the recognition which comes about through an association with a great man or woman. Their family connections and friends make them influential. Of this type, the ancient Rabbis said, 'The slave of a king is treated as a king.' But, then there are also those who are themselves great individuals, irrespective of contacts or trappings of office. They have inner greatness. Observe a figure like Henry Kissinger, the only American Secretary of State who even after leaving office is still extensively consulted on international affairs. These people are seen as men or women who were made great not through their office, but rather through the wisdom of their decisions.

The good news is that we can all be great. Great men and women understand that marriage can be difficult, and that sometimes the novelty and excitement can wear off. But far from succumbing to this they work hard to sustain their passion. They refuse to concede that they must find excitement in someone else's bed. They undertake every avenue and succeed in bringing a permanent state of romance into their married lives. And their rewards are immeasurable. They enjoy the most satisfying intimate lives because they have excitement coupled with love and a feeling of loyalty and goodness. They feel good about themselves and good about their partners. They know that they are doing the right thing.

What a man or woman who feels the itch to cheat should do, is immediately grab one's spouse, and run out and do something truly exciting and novel. Undertake something that will even surprise you Remember, your marriage is your life. Don't try to lead someone else's life. You belong to each other. Your responsibility is to look after your portion in life. So make it glorious. On his deathbed, the great Rabbi Zusya of Anipoli was asked why he was crying: 'When I come before the heavenly throne and the Almighty asks me why I wasn't I as great as Abraham, I will respond, 'Because, Lord, you did not create me to be Abraham.' And when the Almighty asks me why I did not lead a life as great as Moses, I will respond, 'Lord, I was not Moses.' But when God says to me, 'Why weren't you at least Zusyah?' what then will I answer?'

4. Becoming desirable again

Since Kinsey's original sex surveys, almost all research has revealed a link between premarital sexual experience and extramarital adventures. The more of the first, the greater the likelihood of the second.   Carol Botwin, *Tempted Women*

Translations (like wives) are seldom faithful if they are in the least attractive.   Samuel Johnson to James Boswell

In the 1960s, society consumed a terrible lie without ever questioning it. That lie was that people love sex so much that we must indulge each and every desire for it. We were also told that however much we indulge, we will never tire of sex. Today, doubtless as a consequence, the majority of the population have given up on monogamy. The divorce rate currently stands at 50 per cent of the population. Of those who remain married, 75 per cent of husbands, and 50 per cent of wives are, or have in the past, committed adultery. Only an 8th, then, of the general population are being somewhat monogamous. But, even amongst them, marriage is not always that healthy. Finally, only a small percentage of the population find ongoing passion and excitement in marriage, and what its rewards are.

But, imagine the kind of marriage these couples have. Author Naura Hayden describes how she was flying to Los Angeles with her close female friend, Helen Gurley Brown, the editor of Cosmopolitan in the US, and how she exudes an aura of confidence and sexiness and all the men around her just can't get enough. When walking down the aisle all of the men turned their heads to look at her. Objectively speaking her friend is not the most beautiful woman in the world, so she decided to ask her what it was about her that men find so appealing. Helen Brown replied that her husband was the most wonderful man in the world. He makes her feel like the sexiest woman anywhere, so she walks and behaves that way.

Imagine what you could have if you would make your wife feel like your mistress. If you put her before everything: your job, career, money, and every other woman. Your wife would be passionately attracted to you. She would feel desirable all of the time. For these are the things that matter. Notice how, in his classical book on infidelity, Tolstoy always portrays Anna Karenina as dressing up beautifully for her paramour, Count Vronsky, even when no-one is about in the house. She has a lover that makes her feel sexy and wanted, so she naturally lives up to the role in her daily actions, even when there is no-one to watch.

Becoming a creator

In one of its most significant and famous pronouncements, the Bible declares that God created man in His own image. From time immemorial, theologians of all denominations have debated what exactly this means. To me, the application of this teaching is in every day life, and its meaning is clear. In the same way that God is a Creator, so is man. Just like God creates and takes life, man too is endowed with that power. I don't mean here having children. Rather, every time we show someone extravagant attention and affection, we make them feel important, and we really and truly 'create them,' and bring them to life.

Our emotions have the power to elicit an identical response. We have the capacity with our minds, our creativity and ingenuity to take our partners and make them feel special and desirable. When a husband shows his wife that to him she is the sexiest woman in the world, this is what she truly becomes. She thinks of herself as a highly attractive and desirable woman, and acts the part. She starts dressing with great attention, carrying herself with greater audacity, and attracts the stares of all the men around her. This is why studies show that one of the principal things that gives away a husband or wife who are having an extramarital affair is the fact that they now take a lot time to dress up, and spend much more on clothing and looking attractive.

You must believe and accept as fact that lurking deep within each and every husband and wife is a deeply passionate, sensual, and sexy being. If the person you are married to has a heart in their breast that beats, and if they are not physically in a coma, then they also have a hidden, rudimentary fire burning in their hearts, waiting to be discovered. For those who do not appear overtly so this must be brought to the fore by extreme focus and the incredible love, affection, and desire which only you can show your spouse. Some people are born extrovert, naturally sexy. But the vast majority are born with the potential to be exciting and sexy. But what it takes is someone to give them the extreme confidence that they are beautiful and should therefore not fear coming out of their shell.

Resurrecting our libidos from the dead

Central to the psychological well-being of humankind is not just the need for a quiet permanent life, but also passion and excitement. What we desire in our innermost selves isn't only sex, but passionate sex. This leads us to a lasting feeling of closeness and intimacy and sexual hunger for our spouse. There is no need to go outside the marriage in order to restore our self-confidence, or clear that nagging feeling. Everything we want is right here. Our spouse just needs to focus on all the beauty we possess and be reminded of how special we are to them. Then they will give us the confidence we need. But it is your responsibility to make this happen.

I can't accept that people's sexual drive just begins to die or that husbands and wives have different libidos. He loves sex, and she hates it. If you like your home and are committed to living in it, you will beautify it and develop an interest in it which renews itself constantly. If , however, you spend almost no time at home, preferring instead hotel rooms, looking at estate agent's pictures or hanging out in your car, you will have far less impetus to try and put things in the house right. If someone's house looks awful and dull, it is because they don't care much about it. Going to your neighbour's house and being jealous because of its beauty is not the answer.

Ask yourself honestly how quickly the TV gets turned on the moment you come home? How quickly do you pick up the magazine or run to make a phone call? Do you in some way make your spouse feel as if they are non-existent? You've got to get the other men and women off your mind and focus all of your sexual energy on your spouse. We must remember that human sexuality is entirely cerebral. Discarding the appeal of your spouse in your own mind has made them boring and monotonous. It is your omission to act. You must be committed to your other half. Or someone else will do it for you.

5. Kosher desires

The fact that you're allowed to marry another woman, in addition to your wife, makes you hesitate about having an affair with another woman.

> Dr Muhammed Sha'alan, commenting on polygamy

Flirtation is merely an expression of considered desire coupled with an admission of its impracticability.   Marya Mannes

You yawn at one another, / You treat him like a brother! / He treats you like his mother! / Then there's no doubt, the fire's out. / A lady needs a change!   Dorothy Fields

When a man steals your wife, there is no greater revenge than letting him keep her.   Sacha Guitry

The word I hate the most in the English language and which is also incidentally one of the most commonly used in today's vernacular is 'relationship'. Once upon a time, the feelings that a couple felt for one another were connoted by 'marriage' and 'engagement'. But now even married people can have a 'relationship'. This vagueness is reflected in the euphemisms people use for today's courting among men and women: 'seeing someone,' 'dating someone,' 'going out.' All of these descriptions are so casual. What does it mean, to be 'seeing' someone? Is it the same as just looking at an object? Is it similar to the way a child glances out a window? The way one looks at animals in a zoo?

All this has lead to a new type of anxiety. I asked a new student I met if he knew a close friend of mine at his college. 'I do know him and I think he's a jerk.' 'Why do you say that,' I asked. 'Because,' he said, 'he's tried for years to pick up my girlfriend.' But was that a crime? Just how serious is 'a girlfriend'? Is trying to pick up someone else's girlfriend as serious as if she were someone's wife? When I confronted my friend with these allegations, he dismissed them saying that the couple in question had one of those on-off relationships for years.

Another woman told me the story of how she invited a man from her college to the College ball and even paid for his ticket. There she was sitting, feeling that it was wonderful to have a partner at the ball, when she noticed that he was completely absorbed by another woman sitting to his right. Ten minutes later, she turned around again and he was gone. They just skipped the ball together. Is that ethical? After all, she was only on a date with him. What obligations, then, did he have toward her? She was very hurt and believed that the man behaved like an animal, but did he do something wrong?

And a former Oxford student now back at his native American University wrote me an e-mail. 'Shmuley, I have an ethical dilemma and want to hear your opinion. There is a girl whom I have found who I am sure is my soul-mate. The most perfect and wonderful woman in the world. There is one problem, however. She is someone's girlfriend. Is it all ethical for me to pursue it? What would Judaism say? I also think she likes me. Does that make my case any better?' In another age, it would have been easy for me to respond that it is totally unethical to come between people who are dating, because back then most people dated in order to marry. But, are matters still that unequivocal today?

The task of outsiders

I am glad to say that marriage is still considered something special. A highly promiscuous male friend told me that although he loved women, all types of women, he would never touch a married woman, even though the opportunity had presented itself on many occasions. 'I don't consider myself a good person, and I could never be married. I just couldn't sustain the commitment. But the fact that there are people out there who do believe and have married, is a great ray of hope for me that there are still beautiful things in this lonely world. And I never want to contaminate that.' If he felt that he was more and more attracted to someone's wife, he would simply imagine that she was near enough to be admired, but other than that way beyond his grasp.

The Talmud lists ten human actions for which God promises a reward not just in the afterlife, but a physical reward in this world as well. Included in this list is he or she who helps to bring a husband and wife closer together. The rules are obvious enough. Never shame a man in front of his wife, even accidentally. Don't call a wife by a nickname which she finds derogatory. Don't try to be funnier than a husband in his home, especially if personality is not one of his strong points. Don't raise subjects in conversation around a married couple that will make a husband seem ignorant in front of his wife, or vice versa. Always try and engage both of them in conversation, as a couple. Allow the woman of the house to look best. And never think of another man's wife or a woman's husband while having sex in order to stimulate yourself. This is supremely unkosher.

Indeed, many stories of the pious Rabbis of old revolve around the great lengths to which they would go in order to refrain from embarrassing a husband in front of his wife. One such story involves Yankel the newlywed, who touched the candelabra, during a Sabbath meal with the great spiritual master, Rabbi Mendel. Yankel's young wife Perel was aghast and berated Yankel for his ignorace. "Don't you know that touching a candelabra on the Sabbath is forbidden?" Asked for his opinion, the great Rabbi Mendel suggested, however, that as the law is a difficult one he would look it up at home. After lunch Rabbi Mendel's own wife queried, 'Why did you lie? You are the one of the greatest Jewish scholars in Europe. You know the law. A candelabra cannot be touched on the Sabbath. Why did you not correct Yankel when he moved it?' But Mendel replied 'Better I make a fool of myself then a husband be made to look like a fool in front of his wife.'

Getting close to a member of the opposite sex

But what should a man do if he starts feeling strongly attracted to a woman that is not his wife? What should a neglected wife do if a man begins to pay her enormous attention, and she finds herself thinking about him more and more? The ancient Rabbis explain: man has no natural desire for things he cannot possibly attain. Such objects do not interest him, and no human covets those objects which are simply outside their grasp. We are not jealous of a bird's ability to fly because we know that such things are totally outside our reach. We rid ourselves of covetousness by accepting in our own mind that that which belongs to our fellow in all justice belongs to them and not us. Therefore, if you understand that a married couple belong to each other you would not dream of interfering. Similarly, we are usually not interested in men or women who do not reciprocate our interest. Convince yourself that you have been deluding yourself in thinking that the illicit person in question is actually interested.

A publisher of adult magazines in Britain explained to me why British porn was very down-market compared to the world-class models that take off their clothes for Playboy and Penthouse in the United States. The average guy who buys an adult magazine here is blue-collar, working class, he explained to me. So if he buys a magazine with pictures of women who are used to being picked up in Ferraris and taken to dine in three-star Michelin restaurants, he's not even excited by these girls because he thinks to himself, "I could never have her." But if he sees a picture of a nude woman whose hobbies are going to the local McDonald's or having a pint at the pub, these are the kind of girls whom he meets on the factory floor, he gets turned on because he thinks that this girl would respond to his advances.

Another Biblical scholar, Sforno, explains the nature of the prohibition against coveting in a similar fashion: 'It makes your neighbour's wealth absolutely unattainable, and by nature, man does not covet that which he knows he cannot have, what he cannot attain'. Therefore, the fact that a man or woman is married sets them apart from the rest of society and ensures that they are not competed for since the pursuit is seen as unrealistic. Stated in other words, if a man meets a woman whom he fancies, as soon as he discovers that she is married, he should immediately cease coveting her since he understands that as a loyal wife, she is outside his reach. Likewise, he respects the commitment of marriage, and he has no desire to take that which by right belongs to his fellow.

Similarly, if we are married we must think of ourselves as being owned and possessed by someone else. We have undertaken serious commitments to our spouse, which puts outside sharing intimacy with a stranger. If we just take the time to contemplate the fact that we are married, we will stop entertaining romantic possibilities with strangers, and instead focus our need for romance with our spouse.

Non-sexual relationships

What if a spouse becomes incredibly close to a member of the opposite sex without actually consummating their attraction in bed? This may seem far-fetched but, increasingly, modern-day affairs do not involve sex. This is especially true of men and women who are colleagues in the workplace. As psychologist Bonnie Eaker Weil states in her book on adultery 'In fact, these 'affairs of the heart' can be even more treacherous than the purely physical kind. Women, particularly, are inclined to leave their husbands when they feel a strong emotional bond with another man. This is especially likely if they did not marry for love or if they want to get out of a marriage but don't know how. Any activity or relationship that drains too much time and energy from life with your partner is a form of unfaithfulness. That may include workaholism, obsession with children, sports or gambling addiction, as well as emotional liaisons.'

The best way to determine if your are becoming too close to your friend is to focus honestly on the amount of time we think about that friend. If you are married and invent excuses or unimportant reasons to see them, the alarm bells should be going off in your head. This isn't healthy. Your thoughts should be about your spouse and family. Not about a stranger with whom you have every right to share your time, but not be obsessed about. If you're staying at work later than you have to with precious little to do save be with an office associate who is a close friend, you should be going home to your spouse. When travelling on business, you should feel lonely. A husband should miss and need his wife, and a wife should pine for her husband. If it is to hard to bear than you should not be travelling that much. If travelling is part of your job, and you feel the need for illicit male or female companionship because of loneliness, then go and get a different job. Put your spouse first, always!

6. Children, yes or no?

Jews were too busy having children to bother with sex.
World of Shalom Aleichem

Sow your wild oats on Saturday night, and pray for a crop failure
on Sunday. Anonymous

Many people refrain from having children, especially in the early
years of marriage, for reasons, which they claim, are not selfish.
They want an opportunity to get to know each other better before
their children command all their attention. How can they enjoy
sex on the dining room table when the baby is crying, the toilet is
overflowing from Barbi dolls flushed down the pipes, and the kids
come running into the bedroom at the worse possible moments,
forcing Mom and Dad to deliver the most outlandish explanations
as to why they are huddled together with no clothes on. 'It's OK,
Mikey. Go back to sleep. Daddy was just playing the new interac-
tive Tarzan game on your Nintendo with Mommy.'

But how right are they?

When we get married we think we know what love means. But,
in fact, we have no idea what lies in store for us. The principal
problem with romantic relationships and marriage is the tenuous
and ephemeral nature of the emotion. The man who seemed so
mature and sexy now seems like a dirty beast the moment you
first do his laundry. The woman you couldn't live without yester-
day is the same woman you find impossible to share a room with
today. The man who set your heart on fire leaves you all cold once
you have witnessed his selfishness this week. The love is still
there, but where did the intensity go? At this stage we haven't got
a clue that children will revive our passion. And those who wait
stand a good chance of never finding out.

What children teach us

Children increase our freedom. They expose us to their innocence,
by giving us their unconditional trust. When we come home from

work with the entire world's problems on our shoulders and discover our children, oblivious to all the earth's heartache, happily awaiting our return, we are instantly reminded of the truly important things in life. And through that innocence we find the strength to confront the world and all its turmoil once again. Children, then, release us from the tyranny of unimportant everyday concerns and allow us to put things in perspective.

When our children run up to us screaming, Mommy, Daddy, and shower us with hugs and chit chat about their day at school, we are immediately released from the enslavement of job, financial security, and the pursuit of the recognition of our peers. Here, in our children's arms, we find all that we need and are given the inspiration to carry on another day. Our kids couldn't care less where we work or what we earn, and all they really require is our time and attention. We look at our children and say to ourselves that so long as they are healthy, nothing else matters.

Of course, children can be spoiled, noisy and bratty, but they are not vindictive and we therefore feel no slight or insult. Even when they ask why you are so fat or short, something that coming from an adult would be painful, it will cause you to chuckle. You'll understand that they are just being curious about you and about words, and that they are certainly not looking to put you down.

The impatience of children

Some people may counter that children are not all a blessing in disguise. They are too demanding, wanting everything immediately. But I would respond that they fail to see the blessing inherent in a child's lack of patience. Children still live within a primordial state of innocence where something good which is promised materialises immediately. Still inhabiting Eden, they know no death or disease. In their world Mummy and Daddy will never leave them, never fight, and never divorce.

We may call this world an illusion, but we cannot fault children for having this outlook. Who says that the world of reality which we inhabit and which we have created, is so much superior? Through our realisation of this our children teach us patience and kindness. In fact, often when someone asks my advice about the person they are dating, I tell them to see whether they like children. If they show impatience, this reflects not only their self-centredness, but this also suggests that they have little of the innocence required in a passionate relationship.

In marriage, most importantly, children also teach us how to love someone immutably and endlessly. We may feel annoyed with our children, proud or betrayed, but we can never stop loving them. Even the most selfish person can still put his child before him, for when he looks his child in the eye he sees part of himself. Not to love his child would mean not to love himself. He won't see whether his child is fat or ugly, for it is still his own flesh.

Learning this lesson early is crucially important for married couples. Through our children we learn to focus on the unbreakable and unwavering affection that we feel for our spouse. It is fair to say that for most people, prior to having children, they have never tasted of unconditional love. When a man looks upon his wife not just as the woman he loves but as the mother of his children, he begins to love her unconditionally, the way he loves the child whom he has created with her. He extrapolates beyond the unconditional love he feels for his children, and superimposes this on the source of their life, his beautiful bride. Similarly, when his wife looks at her baby she sees her husband's features endearingly reflected in her child's face, and a far deeper mutual love between the two is excited. Together they have created something which is forever a statement of the love felt for each other and continue to feel for each other. The ancient Rabbis say that the Bible's pronouncement of the love between husband and wife making them into one flesh finds its literal realisation in the birth of a child, which is the actual fusion of man and woman. Far from hampering the romantic love between parents who wish to be lovers, our children immeasurably enhance it.

7. Do the children come first?

Kath: Can he be present at the birth of his child?
Ed: It's all any reasonable child can expect if the dad is present at the conception.   Joe Orton, *Entertaining Mr Sloan*

I always wanted to spend more time with my kids. Then one day I did.   Anonymous

At least twice a year my wife and I try and get away alone,

without the children, even just for a weekend or a few days. Having no family in the UK, however, we are forced to have a friend or an au pair look after our five young children while we are away. This scandalises my more religious friends. How could we leave the children with strangers? Some would even ask, how could we leave the children at all? They are obsessed with putting the children first, and I know of many mothers who pride themselves on having never left their children in the care of a babysitter. They'd rather die than do what we do.

Marital love comes first

I think, however, that they are making a mistake born of a misconception of what contribution parents are meant to make to the lives of their children. Parents, and not children, must always come first in marriage. Children should not be allowed to invade the private space of spouses as a couple. They should not come running into their parents' bedroom every five minutes and as a general rule should not sleep in their parents' bed. When children invade their parents' bedroom at night as a matter of habit, their bedroom ceases to be a love-chamber, becoming a family sitting room instead. Children must learn that their parents are related not only through having children together, but also through being husband and wife. It is imperative that the children know that Mommy and Daddy love each other deeply.

Those who put their children before one another, nonetheless, feel that they are better parents. They think that the principal role of parents is to give their children love, time, guidance, patience and security. Not surprisingly, they are also the parents who find their children interfere with their role as lovers. But their marital exhaustion is to them a badge of pride. Don't get me wrong. No doubt their aims are all part of the stew for the successful rearing of children. But to think that these are superior reasons is a mistake.

Children most of all need optimism

But ultimately they fall far short of what it really takes to raise a stable child. Even if parents are the most loving in the whole world, and even if they never leave their children's sight, always bestowing upon them love and attention, the child will still not be happy nor satisfied. Their omnipotence will cease under the child's desire for the fawning love of a member of the opposite sex, as we discussed earlier. Nothing can legislate against that. This is proof that love and security are not the first items which parents must impart to their children, because eventually the child will no longer be satisfied with parental love. Parental love is certainly essential in instilling confidence within the child's personality. But, ultimately it is not enough.

What parents must give their children above all else is *hope*, a sense of optimism for the future that things really work in this world; that happiness, love, companionship, and friendship are not illusory, but achievable goals which they, the children, will one day attain as well. And when he or she looks at the parents, the best thing they can give is be a constant and living reminder that their love for each other will one day be their lot as well. The most important thing that parents can give their children, therefore, is a stable marriage. When child looks at Mom and Dad and sees how happy they make each other, he or she is given hope for their own future that one day they too will marry and be happy. This way the child looks forward to life, rather than being afraid of growing up.

Becoming a better parent

I remember seeing a poll which said that 92 per cent of all parents wanted their children to have a better life – both in terms of material prosperity and finding meaning – than they themselves have had. Well, the best way to do this is to show how you make each other happy. It is vital that you show your mutual adoration and that you put your marriage first. This does not mean to say that we should ever ignore or neglect our children. Rather, it simply means that there must be regular and frequent times which Mommy and Daddy reserve for themselves as lovers, and into which the children cannot intrude. The children will be happy that you take this time, and will await you smilingly upon your return.

Therefore, if you who worry whether you can leave the children for two or three weekends a year (not more though), do it for them. Let them look forward to being married. Let them see two parents who always make each other feel special and loved. Don't make the mistake that giving love is most crucial, for you won't be able to sustain it once they grow older. Optimism is more than enough.

Part Five

Kosher Sex: a Recipe

1. Jealousy

He who loves without jealousy does not truly love
                              The Zohar, 13th Century

[After discovering his wife's infidelity] Bullaro felt for the first time
in his marriage that Judith was no longer his ... Though she was
cheerful around the house... she seemed preoccupied with her
private thoughts, and at night instead of going to bed with him she
stayed up late reading ... Suddenly and ironically, she was becoming the kind of woman he had long idealised in his fantasies – the
daring carefree sexually liberated woman he had searched for ...
                              Gay Talese, *Thy Neighbour's Wife*, 1981

The way to hold a husband is to keep him a little jealous; the way
to lose him is to keep him a little more jealous.
                                          H.L. Mencken

Some of my most interesting table conversations revolve around
the issue of whether jealousy has a place in marriage. On the
whole ours is a generation that interprets jealousy and posses-
siveness as weakness. Spouses say they must be able to taste
freedom. Husbands, having always hated jealous wives, feel they
must be able to flirt with whomever they like, even if they are
always faithful. And women no longer look admiringly at jealousy
in their husband as a sign that he still loves her and wants her to
be exclusively his. Many wives tell me they would get extremely
angry if their husbands show even the slightest hint of jealousy.
They see it as a sign that the marriage lacks trust. In fact, trust,
like the word 'communication,' has become one of the by-words
used by marriage gurus of the 90s, to the exclusion of almost
everything else.

Spouse are each other's possession

But marriage is not about independence. Husbands and wives do indeed belong to each other. A husband and wife who are not somewhat jealous are doing each other a disservice. If you want to be free, then don't get married. If you do, don't expect your spouse to be above jealousy. To a limited extent, a husband should be policed by his wife. Men are easily distracted, and their sexual attention span is especially of a short duration. As Dennis Prager says, 'A man's head is like a radar tower. It turns in the direction of every pair of legs that walk by.' He needs his wife to give him that look that tells him that his behaviour at the cocktail party is just not acceptable. A wife who is not jealous of her husband is not keeping him on the straight and narrow.

The same is true of a wife. If she felt that she can do as she pleases – go to the beach with her old boyfriend, go out to dinner with a colleague from work – and her husband couldn't give a toss, she will feel unloved. Her thoughts will not be 'Wow, Hal is so different. Boy am I lucky.' In her heart of hearts she will think, 'Why doesn't he care. Why isn't he more attached to me? Am I still desirable to him?'

Even Bertrand Russell, the pioneer of open marriage, had to admit that his contempt for the power of jealousy had been 'blinded by theory.' When his disillusioned wife came home pregnant by another man, he could not forgive her. In spite of his firm belief in the 'strength of a deep and permanent affection', her infidelity was too much for him. She had become a stranger to him, and he abandoned her. Their daughter, Kathleen Tait, pithily remarked: 'Calling jealousy deplorable had not freed them from it... both found it hard to admit that the ideal had been destroyed by the old-fashioned evils of jealousy and infidelity.'

Jealousy rekindles the marital flame

The BBC once asked me to debate a writer on sex and relationships who was sharply critical of my views on marriage. When we both got on the air, she immediately attacked me. 'My sister and I were always jealous of each other. We were competitive throughout our lives and it completely ruined our relationship.' I replied: 'You cannot compare the watery love of sisters with the fiery love of marriage. Jealousy is damaging to the love of sisters because theirs 'is not a passionate relationship. Their relationship needs a calm, predictable love which never wavers. But the throes of jealousy to a limited degree are very necessary for the fiery nature of romantic love which thrives on occasionally having petrol thrown on the flames.'

Sometimes in life we only appreciate that which has been lost and rediscovered. And in marriage too we sometimes need to be reminded of the possible loss of those we hold most dear in order to appreciate them further. The problem with every long-term relationship is that excessive familiarity often makes us forget what our spouse truly means to us. When we harbour a limited fear of losing our spouse, or the fear that they find someone more charming, we are instantly reminded of just how precious they are, and we refrain from taking them for granted.

Moreover, in jealousy we are reminded of our spouse's attractiveness and desirability. Since we live with our spouse day in and day out, we often become immune and forgetful of their charm. A man who lives with his wife often forgets to see the woman in her. But when he takes his wife and his best friend out to dinner, there is a moment at which his friend peers into the woman in his wife. It can be a small thing. Perhaps your wife bends over and her bra strap shows for just a second. But your friend catches that. Or he stares at her too intently or just for a moment too long. A husband must capture that moment, must see his wife's attractiveness through someone else's eyes, in order to be reminded of her femininity.

The human condition

The Zohar, Judaism's foremost work of mysticism, declares that the world is broken and man must try and repair it. Until God Himself adds the finishing touches to our imperfect world, there shall always be incompatible opposites, antithetical forces, which govern our lives and our Universe. By nature, therefore, men and women are largely incompatible. Not withstanding how loving and caring a couple may be, it is still impossible for a man to completely understand a woman, or for a woman to completely understand a man. She shall always remain an enigma to him, and they will inevitably be pulled in different directions, destined to vacillate endlessly between love and boredom.

It is not healthy, nor natural, for marriages to settle into routines and patterns that are dull. To an extent, a slight volatility is necessary for a marriage. So that it flickers like a flame. And those couples who don't have an occasional, pleasant earthquake, will see their passion quickly dissipate into the quicksand of everyday routine. Marriage should be a constant wooing. A man becomes infatuated with a woman. She wisely refuses to submit easily and remains just outside his grasp. He now must have her, desiring to spend his life with her. And when he finally does, he quickly tires of her and looks now for the next conquest. Along comes jealousy, reminding him that if he takes her for granted, she has the power to chose and that there are plenty of other people who are (more) interested in her, and the cycle begins again. Jealousy, then is essential in restarting the necessary cycle of marriage in which a husband and wife capitulate to each other but are then, once again just outside each other's hold.

A major problem with jealousy recapturing the spark in marriage is that it entails the spouse who harbours the jealousy experiencing deep pain as well. As we begin to recognise how our spouses are very desirable to members of the opposite sex, and how they too are naturally attracted to other men and women – commensurate with the degree to which we have neglected them – we cannot help but feel inadequate. We begin to feel plagued with insecurity. On what points can we not compete with the others who are interested?

In this respect, Shere Hite made an important discovery in her book on male sexuality. The vast majority of men, she writes, do not marry the women to whom they feel sexually most attracted. They date a woman like this but end up marrying someone with whom they have more in common. They end up putting compatibility before attraction. When I interviewed her about this conclusion and asked her why, she said that this was just another example of the patriarchal society and that men want women whom they can dominate and control. But I think she ignored the constant unhappiness that such a woman would cause us, and the fact that we are not willing to put up with that. Men, with their natural competitive instinct, are afraid of not being good enough and often resist marrying a woman whom they feel they cannot possess completely. It is a feeling of inadequacy rather than patriarchy which motivates their choice.

The male response

Erica Jong describes these tensions perceptively in *Fearless Flying* where Bennett, Isadora's husband, lacks fire in his soul and Isadora feels neglected and bored. However, this changes when he discovers that Isadora is interested in Adrian, an Englishman whom she meets at a conference. "That Englishman you were talking to ... he was really crazy about you." ... He was drawing me toward him and starting to undress me. I could tell he was turned on by the way Adrian had pursued me. So was I. We both made love to Adrian's spirit. Lucky Adrian.' Later, when Bennett finds Isadora in bed with Adrian after all, instead of becoming abusive, he jumps into bed and makes passionate love to her.

We should never have an affair or be unfaithful to our spouse. That is deeply sinful and causes irreconcilable pain to the man or woman we most love. It is unforgivably selfish. But neither should we go to the opposite extreme of never perceiving the extent to which our own spouse is attractive to and attracted by strangers. As with sexuality we must remind ourselves that jealousy is a construct of the mind and not of one's instincts. Whatever we see, we'll find. A friend who is a playwright once told me that after an affair she was dissatisfied with her husband (who knew about the affair), particularly with the size of his appendage. A few months later she rang me, bewildered, that her husband was having an affair with an extremely sexy woman.

There are few things as sexy and rejuvenating to a marriage – yet also deeply painful – as watching one's spouse become the object of desire to a member of the opposite sex. Husbands who were totally wrecked by their wives' infidelity, were also able to renew a very passionate sexual affair with them, that is, if they decided to keep their marriage going. The solution is for jealousy and trust to coexist within the marriage. We must trust our spouse that they always remain devoted to us and will never betray their marriage vows. Nevertheless, we must understand that this trust is based on their affection for, and devotion to us, and not on the fact that they do not desire anyone else intrinsically, or that they are undesirable to someone else. In marriage we must always be aware of the fact that our spouse's fidelity is based on their *choice*, rather than on any lack of desirability to strangers. Indeed, they are very much wanted by other people. Which just reminds us how we must work to ensure that our marriages are always rich and passionate so that our spouse never feels the need to find excitement outside the matrimonial bed.

2. Mystery

The prettiest dresses are worn to be taken off.
> Jean Cocteau (1891-1963)

Love ceases to be a pleasure when it ceases to be a secret.
> Aphra Behn

The glory of the daughter of a king is found specifically in her inward beauty.
> Psalmist lyrics

I firmly support the Judaic belief in society maintaining differing gender roles for men and women. I am fully conscious of the fact that this is the ultimate feminist heresy, but don't misunderstand me. I believe that women are just as capable as men, and that they should be whatever they most fancy – doctors and lawyers, presidents and prime ministers, corporate chairmen and business consultants. Or full-time mothers and wives, if that's what they prefer. Judaism insists that every individual maximise their potential and the ancient Rabbis even maintained that women had greater wisdom than men as well as a more intuitive and deeper spirituality.

But with society increasingly closing the gender gap, and with the stereotypical aggressiveness of the male role having become predominant for both women and men, I believe that the sexes are no longer as attracted to one another as they once were. Indeed, men and women are becoming indistinguishable from one another. They dress the same, discuss the same subjects, pursue the same careers, and thrive in life outside the home. A recent poll in the United States showed that 94 per cent of University graduates would only marry someone with a similar standard of education. Today, there is little besides anatomical differences which throws a veil of mystery between man and woman.

The consequence of a loss of mystery

This urge to harmonise the sexes is what I believe constitutes an important reason for the high rate of divorce. It bores men and women. Without any readily appreciable difference they loose their interest in crossing the divide. Why else bother to make sense of the opposite sex, if sex is the only form of difference and there is nothing to be gained from the different perspective of a male or a female? If compatibility is really more important than attraction, if passion for someone else adds so little to our lives we might as well all not struggle to redeem a dying marriage and just get it all over with.

Because Judaism does not believe in this, The Rules of Judaism (preceding *The Rules* by Ellen Ferrie and Sherrie Schneider, a huge bestseller in the US and the UK) were designed towards realising the separateness of man and woman throughout the centuries. What men and women can give each other is their precious gifts of masculinity and femininity, respectively, which by far transcends mere physiological and anatomical differences. These rules insist that men and women dress differently, pray separated by a divider called a 'mechitza,' and that women never be thrust too far into positions of great exposure which might rob them of their natural mystery. (For this reason I am against co-educational schools.) In this manner, Judaism has tried to ensure that relationships, intimacy and passion will continue to thrive in society. Sex must always be a journey of seduction, a process of discovery, rather than a reachable goal or an attainable destination.

The mystery of women

The great attraction of a woman is specifically her mysterious and elusive properties, the part of her that no man can possess. The Talmud points out that anatomically, men are naturally revealed, while women are hidden. In the genital region, in men everything hangs out, while with women everything is naturally covered and out of sight. With men life is about external projection. With women it is about internal dignity. This is what makes women so great a prize: their natural mystery and secrecy. Any wife who allows herself to be treated as if she is owned by a husband not only runs the risk of compromising her dignity, but also risks bringing stultifying boredom into her marriage. Playing hard-to-get is essential if we want to retain sexual passion.

This is why modesty is so central to sexual passion. Modesty invites fantasy. A man only wishes to undress a woman physically after he has undressed her mentally. Modest dress between husband and wife, even in the privacy of the bedroom, ensures that the body always retains its erotic mystique. Eros is central to a marriage, and the difference between straight sex and eroticism is the extent to which the mind is employed in the sexual routine. Sex which lacks fantasy quickly becomes tiresome. But sex which leaves room for fantasy and mystery is an endless journey. The mind is our only organ which invites and constructs endless possibilities. No man should ever master or fully possess his wife, either outside but especially inside the bedroom.

In Judaism, those things which are holy and special are always somewhat veiled. In the Synagogue, the Torah scrolls are housed in a chamber which is covered first by doors, then by a curtain, and then by an iron gate. When Moses first encounters the divine presence in the burning bush, the Bible records his first reaction as turning away his face. Modesty is the proper reaction to encountering something holy. Indeed, the prophet Isaiah records that every angel has six wings, two with which to fly, two with which to cover its face, and two to cover its feet. The body too must be covered up, unless it is time for sex. This ensures that when a wife does finally undress, her actions invoke the necessary response and her husband becomes hungry to taste of her delights.

Women are not Rabbis and do not serve in overtly public roles in orthodox Judaism because God has given them the beautiful gift of the feminine mystique that makes them the object of male desire. This mystique does not thrive in the spotlight and therefore women are not accorded the spotlight in Jewish rituals and ceremonies. Some would dismiss this as focusing too much on women as sexual objects. This is mistaken. Rather, it arises from a belief that what women carry above all else is an innate feminine dignity which, unlike the male ego, does not necessitate, nor flourish through, being overly exposed. The Zohar says that this is what the great Biblical heroin Ruth meant when she asked Boaz why he had shown her recognition, when she was just a stranger to him. The way the verse should be read is this: how can you Boaz, a man, claim to know me when I, Ruth, a woman, am ultimately unknowable? Do not patronise me by claiming to know me for I am forever mysterious.

3. Romance

> It's most dangerous nowadays for a husband to pay attention to his wife in public. It always makes people think that he beats her when they're alone. Oscar Wilde

> There was once an English nymphomaniac. She simply had to have a man every six months. Anonymous

I once sat with nine sex and relationship experts and therapists at a BBC radio discussion on Valentine's day on the subject of romance and sex in marriage. The presenter went around the room asking each of us how we would define romance. There emerged a quizzical look on the faces of the participants. The question was greeted with a few inaudible mutterings about gestures which show love, like buying flowers or chocolate, but almost no one could actually define what romance is. No wonder the presenter then asked how it was possible that a room full of experts could not come up with a coherent definition. Just think of what your definition would be.

Romance is altruism

To me it is this: a romantic gesture is one where the only purpose is to make one's spouse, boyfriend, or girlfriend feel unique. It is a totally non-utilitarian act. It is no more than a gratuitous act of appreciation. A romantic, therefore, is someone for whom love is an end in itself rather than a means to sex, or some other purpose. An example of what is not romance is if a wife's birthday comes up and her husband produces (on request) a toaster-oven or a dishwasher as a gift. Since the husband's gesture addresses the practical and necessary components of their life together, the gift does not make her feel loved. She is given a practical gift, which helps her prepare food or do the dishes.

But when a husband buys his wife perfume, or better, a beautiful piece of jewellery, he is manifesting his love because he buys her something which is non-essential and impractical. His buying her flowers can have only one purpose, and that is to tell her she is beautiful and unique. The statement he makes with this gesture is that simply making her happy is even more important than meeting the essentials of their survival and upkeep. Similarly, taking your wife to the supermarket to go shopping is not necessarily romantic. It's nice to do things together, but buying food is a necessity and as such you had to go with or without your wife. But stopping in the middle of one of the aisles to give her a kiss is romantic, since it was totally unnecessary. It even distracts you from your purpose of acquiring food. It is an act undertaken solely with the intention of showing your wife affection.

Modern romance

On the same radio show described above, a young woman called to tell about a beautifully romantic experience that had happened just an evening earlier. Her boyfriend of five days brought a dozen red roses to her home for Valentine's day, with a card telling her she was the most beautiful thing he had ever seen. He simply handed her the flowers and disappeared into the night. 'Can you imagine,' she said, 'he didn't even want anything back. He just wanted to tell me that he loved me. And then he went home.'

Immediately, all the men in the studio began laughing into their microphones. 'How old are you?' one relationships expert asked. 'I'm eighteen years old.' 'Well then,' he said, 'you can be forgiven for being so naive. He only gave you those flowers as an entry ticket into your knickers.' 'But he went home right afterward,' she protested. 'Well just wait until tomorrow night when your parents are out,' came the response. Amazingly, all the males in the studio concurred.

I have since asked many single men what they thought about this girl. Sadly, they seemed to agree overwhelmingly that most of their gestures are calculated to get sex off a woman, even if they do love her. The prevalence of premarital sex has for them turned romance into a means to an end. For them the altruistic side of romance has completely vanished, because the availability of premarital sex is something which is too good to miss.

Marriage, romance's last stand

And even if every gesture performed by a man today can be, and usually is, construed as a mere inching of his way closer to sex, what if it is not? At the conclusion of each academic year College balls are organised with tickets costing £140.00 per couple. What if a student seriously loves a girl and asks her out romantically. How is she to discern that they are not concluding a tacit deal where she has to reciprocate at the end of the evening? The answer is that she can't which is why many girls don't accept the invitations.

There is today only one romantic thing which a man can do. And this is to ask a woman to be his wife. For when he does this he is showing her unequivocally that he wants nothing from her save to love her and take care of her for the length of her days. With the exception perhaps of the daughter of a multi-million-aire, a woman could not in her right mind attribute a proposal for marriage to any other motivation other than true love. If a man wants her affection, her caring or just sex, he does not have to marry her. In a world of posturing, where men try to undress women rather than address her with love, marriage is still a haven of romance.

For those who are already married, they can bring new romance into marriage by ensuring that a healthy percentage of their actions are designed solely to show their spouse how much they love and appreciate them. In a Jewish marriage, a husband tries to bring his wife flowers every Friday afternoon, on the eve of the Sabbath. And in an age where so much of one's private life is compromised in favour of work and career, husbands and wives must ensure that they go out to dinner together, reserve time for conversation, or the theatre once-a-week, or if they are very busy with children, at least once a fortnight. And on a daily basis, they should try and set aside at least twenty minutes to half-an-hour for uninterrupted conversation about the unimportant parts of life. Just shoot the breeze together and show one another that you like spending quality time together, that you are there to listen to them complaining about the world, and that ultimately, the sound of their voice alone is enough to make you happy. Call each other from work, even for a moment or too, just to tell your spouse that you were thinking of them, and that they are always on your mind.

4. Depth

Was it any wonder that within a few hours the wild rejoicing ceased and a feeling of deep gloom seemed to pervade the slave quarter?

Booker T. Washington, an American Black, describing his freedom at the conclusion of the American Civil War

It is he who has broken the bond of marriage – not I. I only break its bondage.   Oscar Wilde, *Lady Windermere's Fan*

In the quotation above, a newly freed slave boy describes the deeply solemn reaction to his fellow slaves realisation of the immense responsibility of freedom. Unlike animals, humans have the liberty to choose what they want to be and what they wish to do with their existence. The sad indictment of our generation is that by and large we are throwing our lives away. You walk along the street, glance at the news-stands and the shallow news headlines, look around at the cinema canopies and some of the trash they are advertising, walk by expensive boutiques and watch people devoting their lives to clothes and fashion, walk into a men's room or ladies room and watch people off the street spending huge amounts of time fixing themselves up in the mirrors before they re-emerge into the world. And then it hits you. What has become of my life?

This is not holier-than-thou power play on my part. I can be just as shallow and materialistic as the next guy. But, there is a big difference between loving money and living for work, loving power and living to dominate others, loving clothes and living to shop. You can't dedicate your whole existence to these pursuits. Increasingly, however, we seem to have less to live for and we dedicate our lives toward the least worthy causes, and slowly the meaning in our lives recedes.

Our warped sense of reality

Statistics seem to bear out the general feeling that ours is a most insecure generation in human history. Divorce, suicide, alcoholism, drug abuse, and depression continue to go up. Why do so many people end up addicted to drugs in an attempt to escape reality? Why are 25 per cent of all Americans on Prozac? Why have over one-third of all American adults been treated for depression through counselling and therapy? Why do we consume so much TV and movies, which only helps us to escape from life?

What we have forgotten is that humans are the only creatures with depth in the whole universe. An animal can be entertaining, but it is always entertaining in a one-dimensional way. A parrot can talk, a peacock can show its magnificent colours, a dolphin can do tricks, and a dog or a cat can cause our hearts to melt by resting their heads ever so gently on our lap. But that is all they can do. When they wake up in the morning they are propelled by their instincts. They lack the luxury of having to worry about what they will do with their day.

Living as strangers

Not so the human race, of which every member is multi-faceted, complex and fascinating. Perhaps, then, one of the best ways by which to determine our appreciation for depth in our lives is to see how much we appreciate people and human company. The quality of our lives should be measured by the quality and quantity of our relationships. But, sadly, modern-day society displays a profound boredom with people. Being in human company is never enough and talking about life has become squalid. Instead, people need to be embellished in order to become interesting, and even then we can only speak to them while the radio is on, the TV playing, we're sitting in a movie together, or we're talking of some rubbish tabloid revelation about somebody else's life.

Dating, for example. The typical way in which a couple will date these days is by taking each other out to the movies. Instead of speaking to each other in order to get to know one another better, a couple will sit together, perhaps even hold hands, and have an artificial story – a concocted fantasy dreamt up in Hollywood – entertain them for hours. After sitting passively for two hours, with virtually no interaction, and watching other people speak on the screen in their stead, they will say what a wonderful time they have had together, and how close they have grown. He may still not know her name and they have barely exchanged five sentences. But that is not important, since they were together when they watched Arnold Schwarzenegger blow away bad guys and exclaim, 'Hasta la vista, baby!'

But the same is happening with our friends. When I was a student at Rabbinical college and visited old friends, it irritated me no end that the people I visited thought of watching something 'together' in order to catch up on old times. I would walk into the homes of good friends to be told, 'Shmuley, thank God you're here. Sit down straight away. The Dolphins are down by one touchdown at the bottom of the fourth quarter and they are now on offence. Now we're now going to see Dan Marino come to life.' Now, I love American football as much as anybody. But I had come to catch up with old friends, not to catch up with our favourite football team.

Modern life has become speechless

Today, we can no longer do without the immediate gratification of our senses. Husbands and wives end up speaking about subjects as wonderful as the plumber and the electrician, but rarely about each other. If they do speak about their own personal lives, it is almost always about their problems. Furthermore, with four of five televisions blaring in the house you have to ask, When do couples ever get a chance to speak at all? The International Herald Tribune recently reported that the number one way in which Americans counteract feelings of sadness is to buy themselves a small gift. Shopping for petty, trifling objects can induce happiness and, conversely, when we lose them, it breaks our spirits. Even a scratch on our new car can make us as unhappy, God forbid, as a relative's illness.

We have made human life itself superficial and created a society wherein aesthetics and material wealth quantify the importance and value of human life. 'Women who don't happen to have the physical attributes of a Jane Fonda, a Tina Turner, a fashion model, or a Playboy centrefold are apt to judge themselves harshly as far as their erotic allure goes, often translating this personal sense of body-image deficiency into tangible sexual behaviour patterns. In recent years, many males have been smitten with a similar malady – unless they literally can measure up to the physical appearance of Sylvester Stallone or Brad Pitt, they feel unattractive and thus somehow deficient as lovers. While there were undoubtedly some young men in the 1940's who desperately wanted a physique like Johnny Weissmuller's or Buster Crabbe's, the matter just didn't seem as inexorably linked to sexual appeal.'

This accounts for one of the strongest reasons why contemporary husbands and wives do not love each other as intensely as of old, and do not connect as closely, remaining strangers to each other. Their infinite depth as human beings is closed off to each other. We can pretend that relationships today are no different to one hundred years ago, and that people back then would have divorced just as much, had it not been so stigmatised. But are we really going to fool ourselves into believing that in an age where there was no television, and husbands and wives actually conversed much more with each other, that this did not make them know each other better and feel more closely linked? Shallowness and superficiality are the scourge of marriage, destroying intimacy and passion by covering over the full colour and magnetism of the human soul.

This is why, in strengthening our marriages and relationships, we must focus on enlivening our personalities and ennobling our character. Time was when a man, before going on a date, would practice memorising lines of poetry in order to impress the woman he loved. Today, he will put four hours into fixing his hair and matching his clothes. We must begin to focus more on the depth of personality and assure that our deepest selves are at least as attractive as our outer body. In pursuit of this goal, spiritual values, shared between two loving adults, pulls a couple together with something wholesome and eternal. Praying together, visiting disabled individuals, and even just visiting your respective grandmothers, makes you feel good about yourselves and about each other. Studying together and discussing important personal and religious issues brings out the full vibrancy and brilliance of the human spirit. We must seek to be as colourful on the inside as we are on the outside.

Three ways to resist these temptations

Human life is infinitely precious and cannot be quantified, and in particular the beauty of life lies in its mystery. When a superficial world measures people by what they possess, and marriage and love become conduits to obtaining material possessions, then we have lost the preciousness of life.

(1) We must always involve the emotions when we have sex. When sex involves the emotions, it becomes a spiritual experience which penetrates the superficiality of the flesh in more ways than one. And because it is deep, it allows us to bond with our partner in a way which is satisfying and eternal, rather than the tenuous pubescent types of romance which are all passionate one day, and sputter out the very next. The true measure of emotional involvement in every relationship is commitment, because an emotion without concomitant commitment is a ghost, a disembodied spirit which haunts, but never helps us. Avoid sex which will not lead to intimacy, or sexual practices which will leave you feeling empty when finished.

(2) Modesty and innocence should always be present in sex. Sex is meant to feel good, and this means that first and foremost we must feel good about ourselves. Feeling compromised by a sexual encounter is hardly conducive to full mental and emotional engagement, neither will it allow us to open ourselves up fully in the next sexual encounter. Having sex outside a committed relationship cheapens us and abuses our capacity for intimate communion.

(3) Spirituality must be a central ingredient of a couple's married life. By introducing spiritual values of charity, generosity, kindness, caring and forgiveness into our relationships – as well as a love for children – we ensure that our souls are cared for as much as our bodies. While the bodies of two lovers will always remain separate, their souls have the capacity to rise above their division and fuse together as one. A shared and deep religious belief affords a couple a meaningful meeting point where they both can consecrate their love to a higher cause. Don't be afraid to invite God into your relationship as an equal partner.

5. Friends and family

In 1714, the Roman Catholic Church decided that men confessing the sin of fornication no longer had to supply the name of their partners, as the information was proving too much of a temptation for their confessors.

K.S. Daly, *Sex, A Guide for the Bewildered*

Marriage is a struggle for most people, and a good marriage takes an inordinate amount of time, energy, and caring to make a success. Like raising our children, it is an objective that is of course well worth the effort. Still, good marriages are not easy, and in achieving our mission of having marriages and kosher sex, we can use all the help we can get. And there can be little doubt that particularly advice from family and friends can be an enormous help.

They afford us an external point of release to vent our frustration to someone who is not party to the marriage when doing so directly with our spouse will not always be helpful to the relationship. Contrary to what all sex gurus advocate about the need for unbridled openness and communication in marriage, there are many times in a marriage when is it not healthy just to say what you think, especially when you are angry or frustrated and will say things to your spouse in a painful and non-diplomatic way. Words are eternal and seldomly forgotten.

I know that through a very difficult engagement, which I described earlier in this book, it was only the advice and counsel of a wise Rabbi that my wife and I stayed the course and eventually married. Advice from parents to their married children – so long as it is willingly sought by the children rather than offered unilaterally – is especially helpful since (1) parents are already experienced in marriage, and (2) a husband or wife usually seek to keep their marital problems private and are therefore reluctant to share them with a stranger, but will do so with a parent or other close family member.

Feeling too ashamed to give advice

Nonetheless, increasingly I am seeing that people are refraining from giving much needed guidance and advice to children, siblings, friends, and students, for fear of being labelled hypocrites. People feel that if they are divorced, or have a difficult marriage – if they simply do not feel themselves to be paragons of marital virtue – they have no right to counsel others as to how to behave in wedlock. They'll say, 'My son knows that I have not been a husband and that his mother and I have a bad marriage. If I give him advice he'll just think in his heart that I'm a hypocrite. I guess I have no right to tell him what to do.'

There is little wrong with this initial hesitation. Inevitably, we all face dilemmas in which we want to speak out for what's right, or advise a friend or relative in a certain mode of conduct, but refrain from doing so fearing that we are terrible hypocrites since we don't always practice what we preach. This dilemma is especially acute for writers like myself who give advice to others about marriage and relationships and yet countless times contravene our own advice. Many will choose not to write and advise.

The problem becomes more acute, when people have a false and harmful feeling of guilt about mistakes they make in their marriages. They walk around feeling guilty and culpable for mistakes, and never seem to forgive themselves the errors they have committed. The result is that they give the impression of constantly being unhappy within marriage, when the truth is that they are disappointed with themselves.

Moments before I walked under the wedding canopy in Sydney, Australia, I went up to my mother and asked her to give me her blessing. She herself had had a very difficult marriage which ended in an acrimonious divorce thirteen years later. She took me by the shoulders, and then, wiping tears from her eyes, she spoke words which I shall never forget: 'Shmuley, remember when you were a little boy and heard all those fairy-tales about people living happily ever after? Well, they aren't just fairy-tales. It is perfectly within your power to be a fairy-tale husband and to have the perfect marriage. It simply isn't true what they say, that you have to fight with your wife, and every marriage involves struggle. Unhappiness isn't inevitable. Be the perfect husband, and make your wife feel that she is the luckiest woman in the world.' These words, uttered to me by a woman who had endured a very painful marriage, but had never grown bitter or despondent, have helped me throughout my marriage.

Imperfection does not make one a hypocrite

Perhaps it is soothing to hear of how everyone is a hypocrite. By reading of how great men fall, it removes the challenge from us to have to emulate their greatness. If everyone is guilty of transgression, than we have free license to transgress ourselves. As this book goes to press, the Paula Jones story has put Bill Clinton in the spotlight. He too is a hypocrite, it is said, because he allegedly crudely propositioned a woman but publicly portrays himself as a loving husband and family man.

In a famous critique of Christianity, Betrand Russell writes that Christianity is guilty of believing that man can be perfect in an imperfect world; that personal salvation can precede world redemption. In a similar vein, I believe that our generation is guilty of believing that imperfect people cannot help perfect the world. We assert both directly and indirectly that flawed individuals should remain distanced from public life; that the imperfect man should first fix himself up, and only then should he try and help his community. We make imperfect people feel like they have no right to marry until they first get counselling, and certainly, if a man has flaws he has no right to lecture others about right and wrong.

But a hypocrite is not someone who says one thing and practices another. This would mean that a man who finds it difficult to give charity has no right to encourage others to give, indeed has no right to even publicly declare that charity is virtuous, since he does not himself practice it fully. It would mean that those who lie cannot extol the virtues of truth, and those who are materialistic cannot promote the redeeming qualities of religion and spirituality, and those who inadvertently have a wandering eye cannot extol the blessed qualities of monogamy. The absurdity of this is self-evident. The majority of us are not hypocrites. Rather, we are inconsistent.

What we must aim for is sincerity

In fact, a hypocrite is someone who does not even believe or stand by that which he affirms even while he is preaching it. We are hypocrites if we condemn anger while believing inwardly that only by intimidating one's employees can one get anything done.

We are hypocrites if we extol the virtues of forgiveness but then look down as weak those who overlook slights. We are hypocrites if we commend honesty but look down at those who are silly enough to pay all their taxes, when we advocate the equality of all mankind but look down with contempt at the underprivileged and the poor.

Bill Clinton has every right to advocate family values so long as he is sincere in his convictions that this is the best way to live, amidst his own alleged failing always to live up to this standard. There are those great ones among us who really practice every single thing they preach. But our more realistic goal must be to first always admit mistakes, and never rationalise our errors. And second, to try and pursue what is right to the best of our ability. We are too hard on ourselves. What we should be seeking from ourselves is not perfection, but sincerity. Men and women are not perfect, and so long as they come humbly before their friends and family and admit errors of judgement or action, they should be accorded the full confidence of their loved ones. But they must also be sincere in their efforts to change. In this respect, we must always think of ourselves as *inconsistent* rather than hypocritical.

It Takes a Village ...

Hillary Clinton's 1995 best-seller, *It Takes a Village*, was based around the premise that a whole society is responsible for the rearing of a child. The same is true in nurturing a healthy marriage. I know of almost no husband or wife who at one time or another have not sought or required the help and advice of family or friends who helped them pull through some difficult times. We should not be afraid or ashamed to either seek or offer advice. On the contrary, we must remember that a healthy and happy marriage is essential to a healthy and happy life. And healthy and happy individual members of society lead to a healthy and happy world.

Every community is responsible for offering newlywed couples the support and love they need to see through the difficult times ahead, until this couple too will be ready to assist newlywed couples in their own time. It is for this reason that in the Jewish religion, a couple do not go on honeymoon the morning after their marriage. Rather, for one full week after the wedding, a young bride and groom are entertained by their community to seven days and nights of festivities, thereby demonstrating the support, nurturing, and assistance of the entire community. The young couple are not castaways, all alone in their newly married life.

I remember when I first got engaged, and was plagued by all the usual doubts that accompany the big plunge into commitment and marriage, how a Rabbi whom I was friendly with from Sydney, Australia saw me walking across the street in New York. With callous disregard for his own safety, he charged across the street, ran up to me, and gave me a big hug. 'Congratulations,' he said, 'I just heard about your engagement. You are the luckiest man in the world. I worked with your fiancee' when we were both teachers at a Jewish school in Sydney. She is the most amazing girl. I hope that my own children will one day find someone of such high calibre.' He gave me another hug, and ran off. I remember thinking to myself indeed, how lucky I was, which helped dispel the feelings of anxiety and melancholy that were gripping me at the moment. I also remember thinking what an amazing man he was, a truly righteous individual. One day when one of his children marry, I hope to be able to reciprocate this kindest of gestures.

The Final Word

Climbing the Mountain

A friend of mine called me and asked if I'd join him for a whisky. I extend my free dinner policy to never turning down an offer for a whisky – especially a single malt – so we went to a local pub together. He began telling me how hard married life had been of late. He had been married for 23 years, and it had never been easy. 'We've always had a bumpy ride, but lately it's been a terrible storm. I no longer think that the marriage can survive. We do nothing but argue. We're both miserable. We're now talking seriously about divorce and I'm seeing a solicitor this week.'

I was sad to hear his words. They had three children to think of, and I knew that he loved his wife. I reminded him that as director of a Jewish organisation which specialises in public speakers, I am fortunate to hear approximately one hundred intelligent, and often famous speakers a year on subjects as diverse as the middle-east conflict and the inspiration behind cartoon super heroes. Some speeches are movingly memorable. Others are instantly forgettable. And occasionally a speaker will employ such a fantastic one-liner that one remembers it verbatim.

Such was the case with the American Ambassador to the United Kingdom, Admiral William Crowe, when he addressed the L'Chaim Society at the Oxford Union in May 1994. Admiral Crowe spoke of the difficult times the world was enduring at the time. But as a ray of hope he said, 'At times like these it is important to remember that there have always been times like these.' That line struck a deep chord with me and it enriched my life. 'You've been through hard times before, and you never quit,' I told my friend. 'You've got to remember that you've been down this road previously and you came out married – and happy. Try

to remember what got you over those earlier hurdles. Pick yourself up from your sense of defeat, and never let anything beat
you.'

What distinguishes a period of marital altercation – when a
couple are just having a difficult time together – and the decision
to divorce? Clearly it is this: marital difficulty is when you fight,
but you believe the arguments can be resolved and happiness, or
at least peace, can be restored to the marriage. Divorce is where
you believe that the situation has deteriorated to the extent that
it will never get any better and the relationship cannot be salvaged. Indeed, it will only get worse. Divorce is where you are
convinced that the death-knell has been sounded for your marriage; that the two of you are incapable of achieving reconciliation
or bliss.

In times like those it's important to remember that somewhere
in your life you were in a situation where you seemed defeated; a
friendship that couldn't be salvaged, a business that couldn't be
saved, a school exam that couldn't be passed, an employer that
couldn't be pacified, or a life that couldn't be saved. But you
persevered and you pulled through, and you made it. The first
remedy to the 'no-hope' situation is to remember that there
always is hope. That human beings have an infinite capacity to
renew themselves. That love is so much more powerful than hate.
That sharing life with another life is infinitely more precious than
going it alone. That in the final analysis, even those who have
divorced often remember far more of their loving moments together than their misery or the pain they caused each other.

Success in life is not about victories but about perseverance

Today we have very little appreciation for the quality of struggle.
We want things to be smooth. When they aren't, we believe the
situation to be inherently flawed. That is not the case. Success in
life is not about victories, but perseverance. The great man or
woman is not he or she who triumphs, but rather he or she who
never quits. Marriage is not always about feeling love. Rather, it
is about never ceasing to care. Sometimes when you feel enormously unhappy or hurt by your marriage and your spouse, it is
justifiable not to feel love. When you are hurt, you feel pain. It's

OK not to feel affectionate toward your spouse then. But it's not OK to cease caring and abandon the struggle. A mountain-climber can feel fatigued. As he climbs the mountain, he may sometimes feel that he has no energy to climb any higher. He may feel that the mountain has defeated him, that he is beat. It is perfectly justified then to cease, for a period of time, progressing further. What he cannot do is cease to care and just let go. Because that action of letting go will lead to his immediate fall and destruction.

Life is an uphill struggle. And as we climb the ladder of life we sometimes feel like we have no more inspiration or desire to carry the task forward. During moments like these we must remember that we've been down there before. You've been demoralised before. You've felt defeated before. But the fact that you are still here to remember those previous occasions and emotions is proof enough that you eventually triumphed. Just don't quit. Never abandon the struggle. Because, in the final analysis, life is not about conquering the mountain. Rather, the continuous climb is what existence is all about.

Progressing incrementally, moving painstakingly forward, but never giving up. The mountain of life stretches on endlessly. There is no summit. There is no hilltop from which you can shout victory. Rather, the true measure of success is the distance traversed, how far you have come. Not how high up you are, how happy your marriage is compared to other climbers and couples. You are not them and they are not you. Rather, the mountain upon which you climb is your mountain, it's your life. No-one can measure how much baggage you were laden with before you began climbing. You may have a backpack weighing 80 pounds on your shoulders, while the Jones's next door, whose marital bliss you've always envied, started with a much lighter load.

In marriage it is far better to lose the argument and win back your partner. If you're going through a difficult patch, or even if you're in the midst of one frequent argument, go back to your husband or wife. Say your sorry. Hold them and tell them that they mean everything to you. They may have started the argument. In your heart you may believe, even be sure, that this time they are at fault. It doesn't matter. You go ahead and apologise. It is far better to be in love, to live in peace, then to be right. Go ahead and lose the argument and win back the relationship.

Show your maturity by putting your spouse before your ego or pride.

The earth will one day be inherited not by those who have reached the mountain's summit, but rather by those have never fallen and who have never retreated.

Your marriage is not a facet of your life. It *is* your life. It is not a detail of your happiness, but its central source and greatest blessing. There is enough uncontrollable pain in life without us gratuitously adding unnecessary, self-inflicted wounds. When you feel distanced from your spouse, go and swallow your pride. Go back to the person to whom you once committed your life and exert the energy to make the marriage work again. Apologise if need be, even if you're convinced that you're correct and they're wrong. Love is far more important than being right. Lose the argument and win back your spouse. You loved them once before, so you can rekindle your affection again. By doing so you will have the satisfaction of knowing, not only that you never stopped climbing – that you never quit – but rather that you never climbed alone.

Checklist for Marriage

These are the questions which might together serve as a healthy checklist in establishing criteria for marriage. Now, if the person you're dating meets at least eighteen of the twenty three criteria below – and whether the answer to the questions should be 'yes' or 'no' will be obvious to you – and they are attractive to you, then what are you waiting for? Not everyone will be a shining example of all these standards. But so long as they demonstrate the capacity to learn and better themselves, then they are good people and life-long partner material.

1. Do I find this person attractive?
2. Is this a good person with a good heart?
3. Do they appeal to me, not just aesthetically, but in a deep way, that will last well beyond the first wrinkle in their face?
4. Do I respect them?
5. Do they love children?
6. Do they have the capacity to put other people before themselves and empathise with another person's plight?
7. Are they charitable, not just in pocket, but in person?
8. Are they non-judgmental?
9. Do they live for something other than the material and transitory?
10. Do they share my core values? And if not, do they at least harbour other fundamental core convictions?
11. Are they humble or, at any rate, not arrogant?
12. Are they responsive to my needs?
13. Or do they always demand an explanation for the things which make me happy?
14. When they hurt me, are they forthcoming with an apology?
15. Are they slow rather than quick to anger?

16. And if so, are they at least easily appeased?
17. If I were asked to sum them up to my very best friend, would I describe them as a beautiful person, both inside and out?
18. Do they show an understanding for the fact that the very definition of a relationship is the ability for two people to cater to the needs of one another (even if they do not understand each other)?
19. If you decided not to marry them, how would you feel if you heard that they had got engaged to someone else? Would this cause unbearable pain?
20. If they don't live up to the above standards, do they at least have the humility and capacity to learn?
21. Do they admit their mistakes?
22. After being told them by others?
23. Or on their own?

I put attraction and affection at the top of the list because it would be absurd to suggest that someone contemplate marrying a person whom they do not esteem end treasure, and to whom they do not feel strongly drawn. Furthermore, there must be, in addition to love and emotional attraction, a very deep sexual attraction. But, even emotion is just too ephemeral. It lacks stability and permanence and changes too quickly. If we marry for reasons of love alone, then we have no guarantee that we will feel in the coming year the way we feel now. Love is often based on compatibility or things shard in common. There must be present, therefore, an almost irrational compulsion – an inner inexplicable magnet – which always pulls you towards your beloved. *Attraction* is key, and it is a lot more important even than compatibility. This is also the reason that, notwithstanding this checklist, defining the suitability of a potential partner, the ultimate reason for one's attraction must remain elusive and mysterious. What brings a man and woman together is not what they have in common. Rather, attraction causes them to gravitate toward one another, despite what they *lack* in common. And attraction here is used holistically, to include both the body and, especially, the personality.

Kosher Sex in a Nutshell

Kosher sex is carnal love which leads to knowledge and intimacy. Betrand Russell wrote in *Love, An Escape from Loneliness*: 'Civilised people cannot fully satisfy their sexual instinct without love. The instinct is not fully satisfied unless a man's whole being, mental quite as much as physical, enters into the relation.'[1] Sex at its best, therefore, is an act of capitulation whereby two strangers allow themselves to be carried away to a promised land of familiarity and togetherness. Casual sex, by contrast, is where the two participants stand their ground in the wake of that tidal wave of positive emotion which sex calls forth, remaining rooted and atomised in their own sphere.

Sex for pleasure is an end in itself. But kosher sex is a journey whose destination is a couple who feel joined not only by the same roof or children, but especially through the enjoyment and pleasure which they constantly serve up one another. The fire of sexual attraction and sexual union in the bedroom leads to the closeness and intimacy in life outside the bedroom. Conversely, when sexual attraction is diminished within marriage, the marriage falters in other areas as well. As Masters and Johnson write, 'When things don't work well in the bedroom, they don't work well in the living room either.' Conversely, a man who is not attentive and romantic to his wife outside the bedroom, cannot suddenly expect her to perform inside the bedroom. So, romance and love leads to sex, and kosher sex continues the cycle by engendering continued romance and love.

The purpose of sex is to sew two distinct bodies together as one flesh. When you want to connect the sleeve with a jumper, you take a needle and thread, put the needle through the two separate garments, and even after you later remove the needle, it has become one garment. The same is true of sex. A man and a woman share a very intense, bonding experience which leaves them sewn

together with emotional thread even after they separate. Sex is a
supreme bonding process that has no equal. Kosher sex is where
a man and woman share the most intense evening and thereby
feel themselves to be connected after the sex is over. Movies today
show people having great sex. Great sex makes you feel amazing
and has you howling and swinging from the rafters of the ceilings
together with your lover. But kosher sex is not measured during
the lovemaking itself, but the morning after, when you can't get
your partner off your mind:

> Great sex has you screaming the deity and your mother's name
> during the act. Kosher sex has you remembering your
> lover's name after the act.
> Great sex has you focused entirely on the body of your partner.
> Kosher sex has you bound with the soul of your lover.
> Great sex promotes physical exhilaration. Kosher sex leads to
> spiritual integration.
> Great sex highlights the contours of the body. Kosher sex raises
> the personality up from the confines of the flesh.
> Great sex satisfies a hormonal urge for sexual release. Kosher
> sex caters to a spiritual need for human transcendence and
> fusion with another soul.
> Great sex consists entirely of *motions*. Kosher sex consists of
> motions that elicit lasting *emotions*.
> Great sex is undertaken by two separate bodies, kosher sex by
> two halves of the same soul.
> Great sex is making friction. Kosher sex is making love.
> Great sex is a premeditated and calculated performance. Ko-
> sher sex is the total submission to instinct, freeing the
> individual of all inhibition.
> Great sex is about the interaction of two bodies, kosher sex the
> integration of two souls.
> Great sex leaves no trace. Kosher sex leaves no separation or
> space.
> Great sex is measured while you're in bed together with your
> partner. Kosher sex is measured in the period thereafter,
> when you are physically apart but emotionally close.
> Great sex can often have a man trying to remember the name
> of his partner from the night before. Kosher sex has a man

asking the woman he loves to take his last name for ever more.

Great sex needs many new partners to sustain its passion. Kosher sex unearths deeper layers of the same partner, leading to replenishment and renewal.

After great sex we promptly fall asleep. After kosher sex we fall into each other's arms.

Great sex can be had even while all one's barriers and inhibitions are still up. Kosher sex is humans at their most vulnerable, when their defences are down and their heart exposed.

Great sex is a performance, while kosher sex is an event.

Great sex is a form of sensual gratification. Kosher sex is the ultimate form of knowledge.

Great sex is a delight of the body. Kosher sex is a delight of the soul.

Great sex is an end to an encounter, while kosher sex is the beginning of a relationship.

Kosher sex is the solution to the modern dilemma of sex. As great as the lust for sex may be, the desire for intimacy is still greater. Kosher sex is the kind of sex that caters to this need, because kosher sex leads to intimacy. Kosher sex is passion born of romance. Kosher sex is strong and intense motions that elicit lasting and unfailing emotions. It provides what the Bible proclaims: 'Therefore shall a man leave his father and leave his mother, he shall cleave unto his wife, and they shall become one flesh.'

References

Chapter 1.1
Robert Wright (1994) *The Moral Animal*. New York: Little, Brown.
(1994) *Sex in America*. Canada & USA: CSG Enterprises.
Chapter 1.3
Barbara Ehrenreich, *Time Magazine* (September 1994).
Marlon Brando (1995) *Songs My Mother Taught Me*. London: Arrow.
Chapter 2.1
Sex in America (1994). Canada & USA: CSG Enterprises.
Chapter 2.7
Shere Hite (1981). *The Hite Report on Female Sexuality*. New York:
Ballantine.
Chapter 2.8
Shere Hite (1981) *The Hite Report on Male Sexuality*. London: Mac-
Donald.
Annette Lawson (1988) *Adultery*. Oxford: Blackwells.
Chapter 3.3
Warren Farrell (1990) *Why Men Are the Way They Are?* Toronto –
London: Bantam.
Chapter 3.4
John Gray (1997) *Mars and Venus on a Date*. London: Vermillion.
Chapter 4.3
Shere Hite (1991) *The Hite Report on Love, Passion, and Emotional
Violence*. London: Optima.
Chapter 4.5
Bonnie Eaker Well (1993) *Adultery: The Forgivable Sin*.
Chapter 5.1
Bertrand Russell (1967) *The Autobiography of ...* Vol. 1. London: G.
Allan & Unwin.
Bertrand Russell (1929) *Marriage and Morals*. London: G. Allan &
Unwin.
Erica Jong (1974) *Fearless Flying*. London: Secker & Warburg.
Chapter 5.4
Erich Fromm (1957) *The Art of Loving*. London: G. Allan & Unwin.